TWELVE ORDINARY MEN

The Lives of the Apostles
Companion Workbook and Study Guide

JOHN MACARTHUR

WITH THE ASSISTANCE OF
THE LIVINGSTONE CORPORATION

THOMAS NELSON
Since 1798

NASHVILLE   DALLAS   MEXICO CITY   RIO DE JANEIRO   BEIJING

Twelve Ordinary Men:
The Lives of the Apostles
Companion Workbook and Study Guide

By John MacArthur

Published in Nashville, Tennessee, by Thomas Nelson. Thomas Nelson is a trademark of Thomas Nelson, Inc.

Thomas Nelson, Inc., titles may be purchased in bulk for educational, business, fund-raising, or sales promotional use. For information, please e-mail SpecialMarkets@ThomasNelson.com.

Prepared with the assistance of The Livingstone Corporation.
Project Staff include Greg Asimakoupolos, Dave Veerman, Neil Wilson.

Unless otherwise indicated, Scripture quotations are from the *New King James Version* (NKJV) copyright © 1979, 1980, 1982, Thomas Nelson, Inc., Publishers.

ISBN 978-0-8499-4407-9

Printed in the United States of America
09 10 RRD 16

Contents

A Word from John MacArthur about
Twelve Ordinary Men

A few years ago, I started teaching a verse-by-verse exposition of Luke's Gospel in our church. When I reached Luke 6:13–16 (where Luke records Jesus' calling of the Twelve), I preached a new series of messages on the apostles. Once again, the response was overwhelming and enthusiastic. While preaching the series I realized that an entire generation had been born and reached adulthood in the years since we had last studied the lives of the disciples. They identified with these men in the same way their parents had done more than two decades before.

Even people who had practically memorized the tapes from the earlier series said they still found the lives of the disciples as fresh, relevant, and practical as ever. The new series quickly became another favorite, and people began urging me to combine all the material on the apostles in a book. I didn't need much prodding for such a project. The book you are holding in your hands is the result.

I have always been fascinated with the lives of the twelve apostles. Who isn't? The personality types of these men are familiar to us. They are just like us, and they are like other people we know. They are approachable. They are real and living characters we can identify with. Their faults and foibles, as well as their triumphs and endearing features, are chronicled with meticulous detail in the Word of God. These are men we *want* to know.

These studies in the lives of the apostles have been a particular delight for me—and one of the most fruitful endeavors of my life. My greatest joy is preaching Christ. Eleven of these men shared that passion, devoted their lives to it, and triumphed in it against overwhelming opposition. Despite their shortcomings, they are fitting heroes and role models for us. To study their lives is to get to know the men who were closest to Christ during His earthly life. To realize that they were ordinary people just like you and me is a great blessing. May the Spirit of Christ who taught them transform us the way He transformed them—into precious vessels fit for the Master's use. And may we learn from their examples what it means to be disciples indeed.

—John MacArthur

How to Use This Companion Workbook and Study Guide

This workbook had been designed to enhance your experience of reading John MacArthur's *Twelve Ordinary Men*. As always, MacArthur encourages his readers to continuously cross-check the Scriptures he's using and grapple with the passages upon which he bases his teaching. In large measure, *Twelve Ordinary Men* represents a directed study of the biblical passages that introduce us to the twelve men whom Jesus chose to be His constant companions.

The content in the book has been divided so that the introduction and ten chapters can be studied personally and/or discussed by a small group in twelve sessions. The individual lessons have been based on the assumption that a reader will desire to review the content in the book and reflect on the implications for his or her own life.

Groups using this workbook for *Twelve Ordinary Men* are encouraged to provide each member with a personal copy of the book and workbook for participation. Leaders are advised that the final pages of each lesson include notes and specific answers to factual questions. These should assist them in lesson preparation.

LESSON COMPONENTS

The lessons in this workbook include the following components:

Biblical Focus—Lists the primary Bible passages to which John MacArthur refers in developing the material in the lesson chapter.

Reading Assignment—Lists the particular chapter in the book that relates to the lesson.

Another Look—A set of questions to facilitate review of the content of the chapter in the book.

Biblical Connections—Questions that focus on the biblical passages related to the particular apostle(s) for that lesson.

Highlighting the Lesson—Questions that will allow you to review your understanding of the central teaching points MacArthur develops from the Scripture.

Lasting Implications—These questions assist you in drawing personal conclusions from God's Word regarding the apostles and their lives.

In addition, you will find:

Sidebars—Thought-provoking quotes, usually taken from *Twelve Ordinary Men*.

Daily Assignments—Five sets of questions for each lesson allow you to personally review the content of the lesson and reflect on the lives of the apostles.

Imitating the Master—The close of each Daily Assignment will allow the participant to engage in one of Jesus' habits: the habit of prayer.

For Leaders—A section of notes and suggested answers for selected questions.

May your life be enriched by the lives of the apostles
and the lessons from the Lord who called them.

The Master Who Called Them

BIBLICAL FOCUS

Key passages from this section of the book: Matthew 10:1–4; Mark 3:13–19; Luke 6:12–16; John 6:60–71.

READING ASSIGNMENT

Read both the introduction and chapter 1 of *Twelve Ordinary Men.*

ANOTHER LOOK

The following questions will help you review the material you read in the book.

1. If Jesus walked by the spot where you are seated right now, what three things would you observe about Him almost immediately?

    _____
    _____
    _____
    _____

2. As you consider the twelve apostles whose lives you are about to study in depth, which one do you already identify with most closely? Why?

    _____
    _____
    _____
    _____

3. In the introduction to his book *Twelve Ordinary Men,* MacArthur makes the following statement about Jesus' role: "The Twelve were personally selected and called by Christ. He knew them as only their Creator could know them (cf. John 1:47). In other words, He knew all their faults long before He chose them. He even knew Judas would betray Him (John 6:70; 13:21–27), and yet He chose the traitor anyway and gave him all the same privileges and blessings He gave to the others" (p. xiii). What observations about Jesus occur to you based on the way He chose His apostles?

    _____
    _____

4. In chapter 1, pages 14–21, MacArthur includes a section titled The Teacher. What primary characteristics about Jesus' relationship with His disciples (as a large group) and His apostles (the Twelve) are highlighted in this chapter?

_____

_____

_____

_____

5. How would you explain the second part of the title of chapter 1 in the book, "Common Men, Uncommon Calling"? Why is Jesus' call an "uncommon" call?

_____

_____

_____

_____

> **B**EAR IN MIND, then, that the selection of the Twelve took place at a time when Jesus was faced with the reality of His impending death. He had experienced the rising hostility of the religious leaders. He knew His earthly mission would soon culminate in His death, resurrection, and ascension. And so from this point on, the whole character of His ministry changed. It became His top priority to train the men who would be the chief spokesmen for the gospel after He was gone.
>
> —*Twelve Ordinary Men, p. 14*

BIBLICAL CONNECTIONS

These questions will allow you to think through the biblical passages John MacArthur uses in this particular lesson.

6. Matthew 17:1–9 is one of the first passages MacArthur refers to in explaining the contrast between the ordinariness of the apostles and the extraordinary opportunities they were given. How does this passage illustrate the degree to which Jesus revealed Himself to His apostles?

_____

_____

_____

_____

7. The heading for chapter 1 includes a quotation of 1 Corinthians 1:26–29. What does this passage tell us about God and His purposes?

_____

_____

_____

_____

_____

8. Beginning on page 3, MacArthur deals with the apparent contradiction between the different "calling" passages in the Gospels (Luke 5:3–11; 6:12–16; John 1:35–51). What four "phases" of their calling does he use to explain the different texts? What does each one mean?

_____

_____

_____

_____

WORD FOCUS

To say He spent the whole night requires several words in English. It's only one word in the Greek: *dianuktereuo*. The word is significant. It speaks of enduring at a task through the night. The word could not be used of sleeping all night. It's not an expression you would use if you wanted to say it was dark all night. It has the sense of toiling through the night, staying at a task all night. It suggests that He remained awake through the darkness until morning and that He was persevering all that time in prayer with an immense weight of duty upon Him.

—*Twelve Ordinary Men*, p. 15

9. After describing the "all night" aspects of Jesus' prayer before choosing His apostles, MacArthur explains the literal meaning of the English phrase "continued all night in prayer to God" (Luke 6:12). What does he point out about the nature of Jesus' prayer?

_____

_____

_____

_____

10. Read John 2:13–16 and MacArthur's comments on page 8. How did this event early in Jesus' ministry define His relationship with the religious establishment in Israel?

_____

_____

_____

_____

1

 CLEANSING THE TEMPLE

During the celebration of the Passover, worshipers came from all over Israel and the Roman Empire to Jerusalem. Because many traveled large distances, it was inconvenient to bring their sacrificial animals with them. Opportunistic merchants, seeing a chance to provide a service and probably eyeing considerable profit during this time, set up areas in the outer courts of the temple in order for travelers to buy animals. The money changers were needed because the temple tax, paid annually by every conscientious Jewish male 20 years of age or older (Exodus 30:13–14; Matthew 17:24–27), had to be in Jewish or Tyrian coinage (because of its high purity of silver). Those coming from foreign lands would need to exchange their money into the proper coinage for the tax. The money changers charged a high fee for the exchange. With such a large group of travelers and because of the seasonal nature of the celebration, both the animal dealers and money exchangers exploited the situation for monetary gain ("den of thieves;" Matthew 21:13). Religion had become crass and materialistic.

—*John MacArthur*[1]

HIGHLIGHTING THE LESSON

These questions have been designed to help you identify the central points MacArthur has made in this section of the book.

11. In the sidebar above we get a picture of the present condition of the "official" spiritual leadership and atmosphere in Israel at the time of Christ. What similarities do you see between those conditions and the present state of the Christian church?

   _____
   _____
   _____
   _____

12. MacArthur explains that Jesus violated "modern conventional wisdom" many times in His ministry (p. 2). How did He do that and what were His reasons?

   _____
   _____
   _____
   _____

13. According to the author's overview of Jesus' ministry, why had "the focus of Christ's ministry therefore turned at this point from the multitudes to the few" (p. 7)?

_____

_____

_____

_____

14. Review the sidebar below. Express in your own words why God chose to use ordinary people, like the apostles, to accomplish extraordinary things?

_____

_____

_____

_____

But Christ knew what He was doing. From His divine perspective, the ultimate success of the strategy actually depended on the Holy Spirit working in those men to accomplish His sovereign will. It was a mission that could not be thwarted. That's why it was a work for which God alone deserves praise and glory. Those men were merely instruments in His hands—just as you and I can be God's instruments today. God delights to use such ordinary means—"the foolish things of the world to put to shame the things which are mighty; and the base things of the world and the things which are despised God has chosen, and the things which are not, to bring to nothing the things that are, that no flesh should glory in His presence" (1 Corinthians 1:27–29). The two-thousand-year triumph of the apostolic endeavor is a testimony to the wisdom and power of the divine strategy.

—*Twelve Ordinary Men, pp. xv–xvi*

LASTING IMPLICATIONS

The following questions will assist you in drawing personal conclusions from God's Word.

15. In the sidebar above, MacArthur makes the statement, "Those men were merely instruments in His hands—just as you and I can be God's instruments today." How would you explain that claim to a brand-new believer who wonders where he or she fits in the church?

_____

_____

_____

_____

17. MacArthur closes his introduction with a blessing: "May the Spirit of Christ who taught them transform us the way He transformed them, into precious vessels fit for the Master's use. And may we learn from their example what it means to be disciples indeed" (p. xviii). What three qualities, at this point of your understanding, would you list as essential characteristics of "what it means to be disciples indeed"?

_____

_____

_____

_____

DAILY ASSIGNMENTS

MONDAY

Read John 1:47–49.

1. Who brought Nathanael to Jesus?

_____

_____

_____

_____

2. What was Nathanael's first reaction to Jesus' background? Why?

_____

_____

_____

_____

3. What did Jesus' comment to Nathanael reveal about the Savior's insight?

_____

_____

_____

_____

4. How did Nathanael respond to Him?

_____

_____

_____

_____

5. How would you have responded to Jesus if you had been Nathanael?

_____

_____

_____

_____

6. Is the fact that Jesus has complete knowledge of you (your strengths and weaknesses, your faith and doubt) a source of comfort or concern to you? Why?

_____

_____

_____

_____

7. If Jesus is not surprised by your attitudes or actions, He will not likely be surprised by what your future holds. How might you entrust your concerns about tomorrow to Him?

_____

_____

_____

_____

ॐ *Imitating the Master* ॐ

Dear Lord, I am grateful for those who introduced me to You,
but I am most grateful that You called me to follow You in spite of what
You know about me. I confess my sins and shortcomings to You today
and ask that You would take care of my concerns about my future.
In our Lord Jesus' Name. Amen.

TUESDAY

Read Luke 6:12–16.

1. What did Jesus do all night on the mountain?

_____

_____

_____

_____

2. What clue do you see in these verses that not all who follow Jesus will do so in the same way?

_____

_____

_____

_____

3. What are the main differences between how Jesus prayed and how you pray?

_____

_____

_____

_____

4. What keeps you from praying the way Jesus prayed?

_____

_____

_____

_____

5. If you only had these verses to go on, what would you know about the men Jesus chose to be His team of ambassadors?

_____

_____

_____

_____

6. Consider your abilities or personality. If you had been one of the Twelve, what word or phrase do you think Luke would have used to describe you?

_____

_____

_____

_____

7. If, as some have said, Jesus spent the night interceding for the needs of the Twelve (as opposed to seeking the Father's guidance about which twelve to choose), how does that make you feel about Jesus' intercessory role in your life?

_____

_____

_____

_____

❧ *Imitating the Master* ❧

Jesus, I'm weak when it comes to prayer.
I can't imagine spending an entire night on my knees.
But I am grateful that Your love for me means
You are continually seeking the Father on my behalf.
How wonderful that is! Particularly today, I am feeling weak
in the area of _____. Thank You that because of You,
I can have victory over that sin. In our Lord Jesus' Name. Amen.

Read Luke 5:17–39.

1. What kind of response is Jesus receiving from those who observe His ministry?

_____

_____

_____

_____

2. Who, exactly, were His opponents?

_____

_____

_____

_____

3. List the specific things Jesus did that He was criticized for.

_____

_____

_____

_____

4. What seems to be the motive behind the criticism Jesus received?

_____

_____

_____

_____

5. According to MacArthur, Jesus' recruitment of the Twelve followed on the heels of this opposition. Why was that the case?

_____

_____

_____

_____

6. Describe a time when you sought comfort from colleagues or family because you were being maligned or misunderstood by someone or a group of people.

_____

_____

_____

_____

7. What can you learn from the way Jesus dealt with the opposition that came His way?

_____

_____

_____

_____

ও *Imitating the Master* ও

Lord, I hate it when people find fault with me.
It seems inevitable, though. What isn't inevitable is that I will
react like You did when confronted by critics. Please help me to reach out
to You instead of striking back at those who attack me.
And, Jesus, give me the wisdom and courage to seek out
those who will support me during such difficult times.
In our Lord Jesus' Name. Amen.

THURSDAY

Read John 2:13–16.

1. What did Jesus do upon entering the temple?

    _____
    _____
    _____
    _____

2. What was going on that prompted Jesus' reaction?

    _____
    _____
    _____
    _____

3. How were His actions received?

    _____
    _____
    _____
    _____

4. Does this behavior on the part of the Savior trouble you? Why or why not?

    _____
    _____
    _____
    _____

5. Based on Jesus' example, when would it be appropriate for you to exhibit physical force or take dramatic action in opposition to something or someone?

    _____
    _____
    _____
    _____

6. If you had been one of Jesus' would-be disciples observing the activities in the temple, what would have been going through your mind?

_____

_____

_____

_____

7. If Jesus walked into your life today, what actions would He take to "clean your house"?

_____

_____

_____

_____

❧ Imitating the Master ❧

Jesus, based on the passage I've read today, You are not meek and mild.
Like C. S. Lewis's Christ-figure, Aslan the lion, You are loving but
You are not "safe." Forgive me for the times I lightly dismiss how
You feel about the issues in my life that are hypocritical or inconsistent
with Your plans for my life. Today I'd ask that You overturn
whatever "tables" in my life You feel are keeping me
from doing serious business with You. In our Lord Jesus' Name. Amen.

FRIDAY

Read Luke 22:39–40.

1. According to the text, what was Jesus accustomed to doing?

_____

_____

_____

_____

2. How would you describe the place where Jesus went to pray?

_____

_____

_____

_____

3. What benefits can you see from taking time to observe what Jesus did by habit?

_____

_____

_____

_____

4. What did Jesus ask His disciples to pray about?

_____

_____

_____

_____

5. How did they respond to Jesus' request?

_____

_____

_____

_____

6 How would the place where you regularly spend time in prayer be similar to (or different from) the Mount of Olives?

_____

_____

_____

_____

7. Who might be those who are observing your prayer routine? What would happen if you invited them to join you?

_____

_____

_____

_____

❧ *Imitating the Master* ❧

*Heavenly Father, if a regular prayer time and special prayer place
were necessary for Jesus, how much more they are for me.
I recognize how He gained His strength and wisdom from You
while on His knees, and this appeals to me. Still, You know how
hard it is for me to make time for prayer each day.
Thanks for this study of Jesus and the twelve apostles
that is helping me maintain a regular time with You.
Continue to speak to me through it in the days and weeks to come.
In our Lord Jesus' name. Amen.*

FOR LEADERS

(Notes and suggested answers for selected questions.)

ANOTHER LOOK

If using this workbook in a group, focus on several of these questions for group discussion in order to ensure that the participants are actually reading the book. After several sessions, you may be able to ask broader questions, or simply ask them for general responses before diving into the biblical content of the lessons.

BIBLICAL CONNECTIONS

MacArthur's emphasis on biblical foundations makes this section the most important in each lesson. Devote the major portion of your time to discussing these questions. Invite the group members to ask their own. Be aware in the first two sessions that you will be covering the same pages in the book. Hold specific questions about the disciples until the second lesson. That will provide incentive for the participants to return.

6. The Transfiguration represents an intimate glimpse of Jesus' divine nature given to three of the disciples. Measured by immediate responses and the events that followed, even this astounding revelation did not have a lasting effect on the participants until much later, when it was confirmed by the Resurrection.

7. Jesus' choice of twelve ordinary human beings as the first building blocks of His church illustrates the larger point about God's ways with us—the honor, power, and glory of the Creator never gets confused with the role of the creature ("that no flesh should glory in His presence"). God demonstrates His sovereignty by working through unexpected and "weak" tools.

8. MacArthur details four different aspects of the calling of the disciples:

   Conversion

   Ministry

   Apostleship

   Martyrdom

9. On page 15, MacArthur points out that a literal translation of the phrase would render it "prayer of God" in English. After explaining the context, he makes the following statement:

   > Don't miss the point: The choice Christ would soon make was of such monumental importance that it required ten to twelve hours of

prayer in preparation. What was He praying for? Clarity in the matter of whom to choose? I don't think so. As omniscient God incarnate, the divine will was no mystery to Him. He was no doubt praying for the men He would soon appoint, communing with the Father about the absolute wisdom of His choice, and acting in His capacity as Mediator on their behalf. (*Twelve Ordinary Men,* pp. 15–16)

10. MacArthur presents a number of passages that record the rift between Jesus and the current religious establishment. They did not know God; therefore, they did not know Him when He came in the flesh. The cleansing of the temple demonstrated Jesus' authority and set the stage for their acceptance or rejection of His claim.

DAILY ASSIGNMENTS

Encourage the group participants to not only read the chapters in *Twelve Ordinary Men* assigned for the next lesson (the introduction and chapter 1, to be read again), but to use the Daily Assignments to review and remember the truth from God's Word you have just discussed.

2

The Men Jesus Called:
Perfectly Average, Outstandingly Ordinary

BIBLICAL FOCUS

Key passages from this section of the book: Mark 3:13–19; Luke 5:17–6:12; John 1:47; 1 Corinthians 1:26–29; Timothy 3:2–7.

READING ASSIGNMENT

Review both the introduction and chapter 1 of *Twelve Ordinary Men.*

ANOTHER LOOK

The following questions will help you review the material you read in the book.

1. MacArthur claims that the men Jesus chose were perfectly ordinary in every way. What examples did he give (p. xii)?

    _____
    _____
    _____
    _____

2. The author noted that Jesus knew the faults of the Twelve long before He chose them. What specific conclusions based on this fact does the author highlight (p. xiii)?

    _____
    _____
    _____
    _____

3. MacArthur writes, "One of the main things that motivated Tyndale to translate the Scriptures into the common language was a survey of English clergy." What did that survey reveal (p. 9)?

    _____
    _____
    _____

4. According to the author, "It's not amazing that He drew so many disciples. What is amazing is that anyone rejected Him" (p. 17). How does MacArthur explain why the masses quit following the Savior?

_____

_____

_____

_____

Why twelve? Why not eight? Why not twenty-four? The number twelve was filled with symbolic importance. There were twelve tribes in Israel. But Israel was apostate. The Judaism of Jesus' time represented a corruption of the faith of the Old Testament. Israel had abandoned divine grace in favor of works-religion. Their religion was legalistic. It was shot through with hypocrisy, self-righteous works, man-made regulations, and meaningless ceremonies. It was heretical. It was based on physical descent from Abraham rather than the *faith* of Abraham. In choosing twelve apostles, Christ was in effect appointing new leadership for the new covenant. And the apostles represented the new leaders of the true Israel of God—consisting of people who believe the gospel and were following the faith of Abraham (cf. Romans 4:16). In other words, the twelve apostles symbolized judgment against the twelve tribes of Old Testament Israel.

5. In the sidebar above, MacArthur claims that Jesus' choice of the twelve apostles was not arbitrary. Explain the significance of the number twelve in your own words.

_____

_____

_____

_____

BIBLICAL CONNECTIONS

These questions will allow you to think through the biblical passages John MacArthur uses in this particular lesson.

6. MacArthur calls attention to 2 Corinthians 2:16 as descriptive of an observable strategy by which God uses people (p. xiv). How does that text relate to the individuals Jesus chose as disciples? To what does this text ultimately point?

_____

_____

_____

_____

7. The author cites Zechariah 4:6 to explain why Jesus chose a ragtag team of imperfect individuals instead of relying on a slick PR campaign or brute force. What does that verse from Zechariah suggest is more important than military might or political power (pp. 2–3)?

_____

_____

_____

_____

8. MacArthur identifies the third phase of the Twelve's calling to apostleship as the moment when they were sent out two by two (Mark 6:7). He says, "At this stage they were not quite ready to go out alone" (p. 4). Read Ecclesiastes 4:9–12 and list four practical benefits of companionship.

_____

_____

_____

_____

9. Compare the qualities for spiritual leadership in 1 Timothy 3:2–7 and Titus 1:6–9. What are the common elements? Based on what you know of the Twelve, are ordinary individuals capable of these qualities? Why or why not?

_____

_____

_____

_____

10. According to Mark 3:14, what was the two-step process Jesus used in commissioning the Twelve?

_____

_____

_____

_____

> ℘ The apostles properly hold an exalted place in redemptive history, of course. They are certainly worthy of being regarded as heroes of the faith. The Book of Revelation describes how their names will adorn the twelve gates of the heavenly city, the New Jerusalem. So heaven itself features an eternal tribute to them. But that doesn't diminish the truth that they were as ordinary as you and I. We need to remember them not from their stained-glass images, but from the down-to-earth way the Bible presents them to us. We need to lift them out of their otherworldly obscurity and get to know them as real people. We need to think of them as real men, and not as some kind of exalted figures from the pantheon of religious ritualism.
>
> —*Twelve Ordinary Men*, p. 12

HIGHLIGHTING THE LESSON

These questions have been designed to help you identify the central points MacArthur has made in this section of the book.

11. MacArthur quotes from New Testament theologian A. B. Bruce to illustrate the practical ways the Twelve assisted in Jesus' growing ministry (pp. xiv-xv). What were those practical efforts by the disciples?

    _____

    _____

    _____

    _____

12. What reasons does the author offer as to why Jesus did not choose His disciples from the religious establishment? What evidence of hypocrisy in religious hierarchy do you see today?

    _____

    _____

    _____

    _____

13. All of the Twelve were Galileans. What conclusions are intended to be drawn from that characterization? If Jesus were to choose "Galileans" today, what people grouping in our culture do you think He would draw from?

    _____

    _____

    _____

    _____

14. The author asserts that Jesus' choice of twelve men from scores (if not hundreds) of followers illustrates what theological doctrine? Why is the word *election* a helpful way to describe this reality?

    _____

    _____

    _____

    _____

15. What three roles comprised the apostles' task?

    _____

    _____

    _____

    _____

WORD FOCUS

Sometimes in Scripture the Twelve are called "disciples"—*mathetes* in the Greek text (Matthew 10:1; 11:1; 20:17; Luke 9:1). The word means "learners," "students." That is what they were during those months they spent under the direct and personal tutelage of the Lord. He had multitudes of disciples, but these twelve were specifically called and chosen to a unique apostolic office. Therefore they are also designated "apostles"—*apostoloi* in the Greek. The word simply means "messengers," or "sent ones." They were given a unique ambassadorial office of authority and spokesmanship for Christ. Luke especially uses this term in his Gospel and throughout the Book of Acts, and he reserves the term almost exclusively for the Twelve. Matthew speaks of "apostles" only once (Matthew 10:2); elsewhere, he refers to "twelve disciples" (11:1; 20:17) or "the twelve" (26:14, 20, 47). Likewise, Mark uses the term "apostles" only once (Mark 6:30). Other than that, he always refers to the apostles as "the twelve" (3:14; 4:10; 6:7; 9:35; 10:32; 11:11; 14:10, 17, 20, 43). John, too, uses the word *apostolos* just once, in a non-technical sense (John 13:16—where most English versions render the expression, "he who is sent"). Like Mark, John always refers to the apostolic band as "the twelve" (John 6:67, 70-71; 20:24).

LASTING IMPLICATIONS

The following questions will assist you in drawing personal conclusions from God's Word.

16. According to MacArthur, why is there such a fascination in one generation after another over the lives of the apostles?

_____
_____
_____
_____

17. The author identifies the Twelve as "real and living characters we can identify with" (p. xii). Why is this significant?

_____
_____
_____
_____

18. Have you ever sensed that you were being used by God as an "instrument in His hands"? Explain.

_____
_____
_____
_____

19. William Tyndale's survey of sixteenth-century clergy indicated that few knew who the twelve apostles were. How many can you name without looking them up?

_____

_____

_____

_____

20. According to the book, the apostles didn't measure up in five areas. What were they? In which of these five deficiencies do you think you would give the apostles a run for their money?

_____

_____

_____

_____

The office of a *shaliah* was well known. *Shaliah* were sent out to settle legal or religious disputes, and they acted with the full authority of the whole council. Some prominent rabbis also had their *shaliah*, "sent ones" who taught their message and represented them with their full authority. Even the Jewish Mishnah (a collection of oral traditions originally conceived as a commentary on the Law) recognized the role of the *shaliah*. It says, "The one sent by the man is as the man himself." So the nature of the office was well known to the Jewish people.

Thus when Jesus appointed apostles, He was saying something very familiar to people in that culture. These were His delegates. They were His trusted *shaliah*. They spoke with His authority, delivered His message, and exercised His authority.

—*Twelve Ordinary Men, pp. 20–21*

DAILY ASSIGNMENTS

MONDAY

Read 1 Corinthians 1:26–29.

1. What does this text reveal about the kind of people God typically uses to do His work?

_____

_____

_____

_____

2. Identify the categories that are contrasted in these verses.

_____
_____
_____
_____

3. How do the twelve apostles' qualify as "foolish" and "weak"?

_____
_____
_____
_____

4. Who comes to mind when you think of unlikely people God has used in your life?

_____
_____
_____
_____

5. If nobility and might are not prerequisites for being called by God, how does that reality alter your assumptions of what God might have in mind for you?

_____
_____
_____
_____

6. What parallel "lack of qualification" similar to the apostles do you see in your life?

_____
_____
_____
_____

7. Based on His track record with the disciples and many others, how does Jesus view your abilities or lack thereof?

_____
_____
_____
_____

◈ *Imitating the Master* ◈

Lord, it's obvious that You didn't call the twelve apostles based
on their education, pedigree, or experience. I am encouraged by that thought.
Open my eyes and my heart to believe that You might call me to accomplish
far more than I ever thought I was capable of. Not for my glory but that the
borders of Your kingdom might be expanded. In our Lord Jesus' Name. Amen.

TUESDAY

Read Matthew 4:18–20.

1. What were the circumstances surrounding Jesus' first encounter with Peter and Andrew?

_____

_____

_____

_____

2. What did Jesus say to them?

_____

_____

_____

_____

3. What is curious about the way Jesus challenged them? How might He have tweaked His invitation to you (given your occupation)?

_____

_____

_____

_____

4. Imagine yourself in Peter's sandals. What thoughts would be going through your head when Jesus asks you to follow Him?

_____

_____

_____

_____

5. What would have been your response to such an unexpected invitation?

_____

_____

_____

_____

6. Describe the moment when you decided to "follow" Jesus.

_____

_____

_____

_____

7. What caused you to respond as you did?

_____

_____

_____

Jesus, I will always remember when You got my attention and
challenged me to turn my back on my old ways and follow You.
That was the beginning of a new season in my life. I'm still learning
what it means to follow You. Thank You for these examples of men
who gave up everything to follow You. Show me what things are still in my life
that I need to let go of in order to follow You better. In our Lord Jesus' Name. Amen.

WEDNESDAY

Read 1 Timothy 3:2–7.

1. List the qualifications Paul identifies as prerequisites for being a bishop or overseer in the local church.

_____

_____

_____

_____

2. Circle those that the Twelve would not have been very good at when Jesus first chose them.

_____

_____

_____

_____

3. How can you reconcile that God delights in choosing ordinary nobodies but nonetheless has high expectations of them at the same time?

_____

_____

_____

_____

4. Which of the qualifications listed in this passage are easy for you? Which are more difficult?

_____

_____

_____

_____

5. What was the means by which the apostles grew in their grasp of these qualities?

_____

_____

_____

_____

6. Since that same growth factor is available to you, in what ways are you following through as a potential leader in Christ's church?

_____

_____

_____

_____

7. In what ways are you selling yourself too short by not expecting God to work in and through your life?

_____

_____

_____

_____

⪔ *Imitating the Master* ⪕

I'm humbled by the thought that You would want to use me, Lord.
Yet, You invested in the lives of the Twelve and as a result they made great progress.
Please help me make strides in the right direction, Jesus.
In our Lord Jesus' Name I pray. Amen.

THURSDAY

Read John 15:16.

1. Based on this verse, who deserves the credit for your being in the family of God?

_____

_____

_____

_____

2. According to the text, for what purpose did Jesus choose you?

_____

_____

_____

_____

3. As you look at this verse, who do you sense bears the responsibility for accomplishing this purpose—you or Jesus?

_____

_____

_____

_____

4. The Twelve were called to produce the "fruit" of evangelizing others, establishing the church, writing the Scriptures, physical healings, etc. What fruit does God want to grow in your life?

_____

_____

_____

_____

5. Looking back on your life as a Christian, what fruit has remained and what fruit is no longer observable?

_____

_____

_____

_____

6. What actions might God want to take with you, as one of His branches, so that you can bear more and lasting fruit?

_____

_____

_____

_____

7. What is the best part, as far as you're concerned, about being a "branch"?

_____

_____

_____

_____

∂ Imitating the Master ∂

Jesus, I'm amazed to think that You determined that I would be part of
Your forever family. I'd certainly be the first to admit that I don't deserve it.
I used to think that I chose You and invited You into my life. I see now that was
wrong. Thank You so much for choosing me. Please keep me humble and dependent
on You. Continue to prune my life and do whatever is necessary to bring
about the harvest in my life that You desire. In our Lord Jesus' Name. Amen.

FRIDAY

Read Acts 4:13.

1. What was it that stood out about the apostles to the people of Jerusalem?

_____

_____

_____

_____

2. What two words describe the "ordinariness" of the apostles in this verse?

_____

_____

_____

_____

3. Although the apostles' dialect was a dead giveaway that they were Galileans (from "the wrong side of the tracks"), what else was apparent to those who witnessed their behavior and their insight?

_____

_____

_____

_____

4. In what ways did being "with Jesus" affect the disciples?

_____

_____

_____

_____

5. What kind of activity would make it possible for those who observe Christians today to be able to say, "They have been with Jesus"?

_____

_____

_____

_____

6. How important is spiritual maturity as one of the measurements in gauging your personal effectiveness or success?

_____

_____

_____

_____

7. What would it take to make that objective your most important measurement of progress?

_____

_____

_____

_____

Lord Jesus, I want others to be able to detect that I spend time with You. That hasn't always been the case, but it is a growing desire on my part now. I'm grateful for this study that makes spending time with You interesting and desirable because of the practical insight it contains. Would You continue to speak to me as I spend time in this book and Your Book? With gratitude and expectation,
In our Lord Jesus' Name I pray. Amen.

FOR LEADERS

(Notes and suggested answers for selected questions.)

ANOTHER LOOK

If using this workbook in a group, focus on several of these questions for group discussion in order to ensure that the participants are actually reading the book. After several sessions, you may be able to ask broader questions, or simply ask them for general responses before diving into the biblical content of the lessons.

1. Not one of them was renowned for scholarship or great erudition. They had no track record as orators or theologians. They were not outstanding because of their natural talents or intellectual abilities. They were slow learners and spiritually dense.

2. From our human perspective the spread of the gospel hinged entirely on these twelve ordinary guys. The training they received was all too brief. They seemed to catch on, but at Jesus' death they bailed out and failed big time. Still, following Jesus' resurrection, they accomplished great feats that have stood the test of two thousand years. They are proof positive that God's strength is made perfect in weakness.

3. Most did not know who the twelve apostles were. Only a few of them could name four or five of the leading apostles.

4. The main reason was because His message was more than they could bear. He chided them for following Him for wrong reasons. He spoke in graphic terms about needing to eat His flesh and drink His blood.

5. The number twelve was filled with symbolic importance. There were twelve tribes in Israel, but Israel was apostate. In choosing twelve apostles, Christ was in effect appointing new leadership for the New Covenant.

BIBLICAL CONNECTIONS

MacArthur's emphasis on biblical foundations makes this section the most important in each lesson. Devote the major portion of your time to discussing these questions. Invite the group to ask their own. Be aware in the first two sessions that you will be covering the same pages in the book. Remember to allow specific questions about the disciples in this lesson that the group had last week.

6. God uses the weak vessels to accomplish His plans in order that His strength is recognized. The apostles were the epitome of weakness.

7. God's Holy Spirit at work within people's lives is stronger than any military or political power.

   • It results in a good reward for their work.

   • If one falls down, his friend can help him up.

   • They will warm each other.

   • There is strength in numbers.

8. They must be above reproach, the husband of one wife, temperate, self-controlled, respectable, hospitable, able to teach, not given to drunkenness, not lovers of money, able to manage their own families well. The disciples proved that you can be ideal without being perfect.

9. Jesus called the Twelve to be with Him before He sent them out to minister on His behalf.

HIGHLIGHTING THE LESSON

10. They provided administrative assistance and division of labor as the numbers of people and distance to be traveled became greater. They ministered to Jesus' daily needs.

11. The religious established repudiated everything Jesus stood for. They hated Him and His message. He was a threat to their power. Since they were determined to destroy Him, why would He choose men from their ranks to serve His cause?

12. Think of Galileans as similar to the people who are looked down upon in your area of the country. Galileans understood unfair discrimination.

13. The doctrine of divine sovereignty. In an election, the person casting a ballot is free to choose whom they want to a given role. That is the way it is with those God chooses. He is under no obligation. He freely chooses whom He wants.

14. They were chosen to be apostles to:

- Edify the church.

- Be examples of virtue.

- Perform miracles to confirm their message.

LASTING IMPLICATIONS

15. The apostles lacked spiritual understanding:

- They lacked humility.

- They lacked faith.

- They lacked commitment.

- They lacked power.

DAILY ASSIGNMENTS

Encourage the group participants not only to read the chapter in *Twelve Ordinary Men* assigned for the next lesson (chapter 2), but to use the Daily Assignments to review and remember the truth from God's Word you have just discussed.

Peter: The Leader of the Lot

BIBLICAL FOCUS

Key passages from this section of the book: Matthew 16:16–23; Mark 14:37–38; Luke 22:31–32; John 1:43–55; 13:4–7; 21:15–17; Galatians 2; 1 Peter 1:3–7.

READING ASSIGNMENT

Read chapter 2 of *Twelve Ordinary Men.*

ANOTHER LOOK

The following questions will help you review the material you read in the book.

1. Mac Arthur writes, "In all four biblical lists [of the apostles], the same twelve men are named, and the order in which they are given is strikingly similar. The first name in all four lists is Peter" (p. 29). What does he suggest that means?

   _____
   _____
   _____
   _____

2. After Christ's first encounter with Simon Peter, the author observes that that there are two distinct contexts in which the name "Simon" regularly is applied to him. What were those two contexts?

   _____
   _____
   _____
   _____

3. According to MacArthur there is an obvious conclusion to be drawn from the fact that "in the Gospel of John, John refers to his friend fifteen times as 'Simon Peter'" (p. 36). What is the author's explanation for why John uses both names?

   _____
   _____
   _____

4. On pages 47–48, the author quotes J. R. Miller: "The only thing that walks back from the tomb with the mourners and refuses to be buried is the character of a man. What a man is survives him. It can never be buried." What six character qualities does MacArthur then uncover in Peter's life?

_____

_____

_____

_____

5. MacArthur writes on page 51, "Leaders are often tempted by the sin of pride." Why is this true?

_____

_____

_____

_____

BIBLICAL CONNECTIONS

These questions will allow you to think through the biblical passages John MacArthur uses in this particular lesson.

6. Note the differences in the various "Simons" we encounter in the Gospels. Look up each passage and write a word or phrase that distinguishes that person as being unique.
Matthew 13:55

_____

_____

John 6:71

_____

_____

Matthew 26:6

_____

_____

Luke 7:36–40

_____

_____

Matthew 27:32

_____

_____

Matthew 16:17

_____

_____

7. MacArthur calls attention to the unique way in which God wired Peter from the womb. He cites Psalm 139:13–16 as a point of reference. What God-given fabric would you say He wove into your personality from the very beginning of your life?

_____

_____

_____

_____

8. Read John 13:36–38 and 21:15–17. What significance do you see in the two texts?

_____

_____

_____

_____

9. Look up 1 Peter 2:21–23. These are words written by the same person who attempted to decapitate a man who was with the party that ambushed Jesus in the Garden of Gethsemane to arrest Him. How does that knowledge affect your perspective on his sincerity? Explain.

_____

_____

_____

_____

10. In 1 Peter 5:8–10, Peter preaches from the pulpit of personal experience. His reference to "sufferings" is not simply for the sake of acknowledging the hardships, temptations, and failure he's faced. What is Peter saying about suffering that has a universal ring to it?

_____

_____

_____

_____

> Peter's name is mentioned in the Gospels more than any other name except Jesus. No one speaks as often as Peter, and no one is spoken to by the Lord as often as Peter. No disciple is so frequently rebuked by the Lord as Peter; and no disciple ever rebukes the Lord except Peter (Matthew 16:22). No one else confessed Christ more boldly or acknowledged His lordship more explicitly; yet no other disciple ever verbally denied Christ as forcefully or publicly as Peter did. No one is praised and blessed by Christ the way Peter was; yet Peter was also the only one Christ ever addressed as Satan. The Lord had harsher things to say to Peter than He ever said to any of the others.
>
> —*Twelve Ordinary Men, p. 39*

WORD FOCUS

"Peter" was sort of a nickname. It means "Rock." (*Petros* is the Greek word for "a piece of rock, a stone.") The Aramaic equivalent was *Cephas* (cf. I Corinthians 1:12; 3:22; 9:5; 15:5; Galatians 2:9). John 1:42 describes Jesus' first face-to-face meeting with Simon Peter: "Now when Jesus looked at him, He said, 'You are Simon the son of Jonah. You shall be called Cephas' (which is translated, A Stone)." Those were apparently the first words Jesus ever said to Peter. And from then on, "Rock" was his nickname.

—Twelve Ordinary Men, p. 34

HIGHLIGHTING THE LESSON

These questions have been designed to help you identify the central points MacArthur has made in this section of the book.

11. Why does MacArthur suggest that Jesus gave Simon a nickname that called to mind a "Rock" (as described in the above sidebar)? What makes Jesus' action motivational instead of a sarcastic put-down?

_____

_____

_____

_____

12. What three ingredients does the author suggest made up the raw material that contributed to Peter's leader-like personality?

_____

_____

_____

_____

13. Leaders like Peter are not just born. They are shaped by circumstances and experiences of life. Thinking back on previous studies or sermons about Peter, what can you recall from his life that tempered him and proved to be part of his education in the "school of hard knocks"?

_____

_____

_____

_____

14. Besides praying that his faith will not fail, how did Jesus equip Peter to "strengthen [his] brethren" (Luke 22:32)?

_____

_____

_____

_____

15. Read Galatians 2. Here Paul (the apostle who was not one of the original Twelve) relates an encounter with Peter in which the big fisherman comes off more as a big fool. Which of the following expressions best captures Peter's behavior? Explain.

    • double-minded mind is unstable in all its ways.
    • Once a Jew always a Jew.
    • Give me that old-time religion.
    • I don't believe in breaking the law.

_____

_____

_____

_____

Did Peter learn to love? He certainly did. Love became one of the hallmarks of his teaching. In 1 Peter 4:8 he wrote, "Above all things have fervent love for one another, for 'love will cover a multitude of sins.'" The Greek word translated "fervent" in that verse is *ektenes*, literally meaning "stretched to the limit." Peter was urging us to love to the maximum of our capacity. The love he spoke of is not about a feeling. It's not about how we respond to people who are naturally lovable. It's about a love that covers and compensates for others' failures and weaknesses: "Love will cover a multitude of sins." This is the sort of love that washes a brother's dirty feet. Peter himself had learned that lesson from Christ's example.

—*Twelve Ordinary Men, pp. 55–56*

LASTING IMPLICATIONS

The following questions will assist you in drawing personal application from God's Word.

16. "If Christ in His perfect humanity could not pour equal amounts of time and energy into everyone He drew around Him, no leader should expect to be able to do that" (p. 31). Based on the author's observation, how would you evaluate the effectiveness of your people management skills?

_____

_____

_____

_____

17. Former Los Angeles Dodger manager Tommy Lasorda emulated Jesus' approach with Peter by giving timid Orel Hershiser the nickname of "Bulldog." As with Peter, it worked. In what ways have others motivated you to actualize your God-given potential?

_____

_____

_____

_____

18. MacArthur calls attention to the fact that most Christians are like Peter because they are both spiritual and carnal. Which of your behaviors and attitudes fit in each category?

_____

_____

_____

_____

19. Peter had to learn a kind of love that he'd not known before. Jesus demonstrated a love that is not based on feelings and is not reserved for people who are naturally loveable. It "covers and compensates" for others' shortcomings (p. 55). When has someone demonstrated that kind of love for you? Explain.

_____

_____

_____

_____

20. In typical fashion, Peter refused to let Jesus wash his feet. Then, in giving in to the Master's demands, he insisted that he be entirely bathed. But Jesus cautioned that only his feet needed to be washed. Here is a picture, MacArthur suggests, of the kind of daily forgiveness (not salvation) that Jesus calls us all to seek (Luke 11:4). How can you go about allowing the Lord to "wash your feet" each day?

_____

_____

_____

_____

There was that famous occasion when Jesus asked, "Who do men say that I, the Son of Man, am?" (Matthew 16:13). Several opinions were circulating among the people about that. "So they said, 'Some say John the Baptist, some Elijah, and others Jeremiah or one of the prophets'" (v. 14). Jesus then asked the disciples in particular, "But who do *you* say that I am?" (v. 15, emphasis added). It was at that point that Peter boldly spoke out above the rest: "You are the Christ, the Son of the living God" (v. 16). The other disciples were still processing the question, like schoolboys afraid to speak up lest they give the wrong answer. Peter was bold and decisive. That's a vital characteristic of all great leaders. Sometimes he had to take a step back, undo, retract, or be rebuked. But the fact that he was always willing to grab opportunity by the throat marked him as a natural leader.

—*Twelve Ordinary Men, p. 41*

DAILY ASSIGNMENTS

MONDAY

Read Luke 6:13–16.

1. Whose name appears at the top of the list of disciples?

   _____

   _____

   _____

   _____

2. What clues do these verses provide you about those who made up the Twelve?

   _____

   _____

   _____

   _____

3. What significance should be placed in the order of these names?

   _____

   _____

   _____

   _____

4. How do you feel about the fact that the apparent leader was such an impetuous person?

   _____

   _____

   _____

   _____

5. In what setting would you be viewed as a leader? When are you most like Peter?

   _____

   _____

   _____

   _____

6. List at least three items of added information you would like to have about the original Twelve.

   _____

   _____

   _____

   _____

7. Why did the Lord limit our information about these ordinary men?

_____

_____

_____

_____

❧ *Imitating the Master* ❧

*Lord, I'm reminded again how ordinary the people who You called
to be Your ambassadors really were. It is insightful to see that You allowed
someone as imperfect as Peter to be the leader of the group. I take comfort in
knowing that You just might be able to use me in leadership roles while
I am in the process of becoming more like You. In our Lord Jesus' Name. Amen.*

TUESDAY

Read 2 Peter 1:1.

1. How does Peter refer to himself in this letter?

_____

_____

_____

_____

2. To whom is Peter writing?

_____

_____

_____

_____

3. Based on the fact that whenever "Simon" is used to reference Peter it is a formal reference or self-deprecating, which does this appear to be here? Explain your answer.

_____

_____

_____

_____

4. If Peter is expressing vulnerability here, are you more inclined to dismiss what he has to say or are you more apt to pay attention to it? Why?

_____

_____

_____

_____

5. Who is someone who has impacted your life in a positive way as a Christian—someone who was not opposed to admitting his or her imperfections?

_____

_____

_____

_____

6. What is a weakness you are willing to admit to others when you are trying to influence them? Why?

_____

_____

_____

_____

7. The fact that Simon Peter used both names means that even though he believed there were still some "Simon" qualities in his life, he was confident that he was also the "rock" Jesus credited him as being. What is a strength in your spiritual life (thanks to the Lord's grace)?

_____

_____

_____

_____

✑ *Imitating the Master* ✑

Jesus, like Peter I'm aware of the fact that I'm a mixture of my old nature
and my new nature. Thank You that by Your grace I am becoming more like You
each day. Please remind me that You are committed to helping me reach
my potential. In our Lord Jesus' Name. Amen.

WEDNESDAY

Read Luke 22:47–51.

1. How did Peter react to the arrest of Jesus (see also John 18:10)?

_____

_____

_____

_____

2. How did the other disciples react at first?

_____

_____

_____

_____

3. What was Jesus' response to Peter's action?

_____

_____

_____

_____

4. In what way does Jesus make a case for His own death by what He says?

_____

_____

_____

_____

5. Peter's action appears to be motivated by his love for Jesus. Can you think of a time when you did the wrong thing for the right reason? Specify why it turned out to be an inappropriate response.

_____

_____

_____

_____

6. Identify some area in your life where you are tempted to "strike out" and defend yourself rather than to trust the Lord's will.

_____

_____

_____

_____

7. How do you understand the concept of trusting the Lord's will? How would you know you are faithfully carrying out that approach?

_____

_____

_____

_____

❧ *Imitating the Master* ❧

I'm more like Peter than I realized. I don't like to take it on the chin anymore than
he did. But Lord, I know that You desire to teach me restraint and self-control.
As I contemplate _____, I am inclined to act in my own wisdom
and try to handle it all by myself. Please give me the
patience to wait on You. In our Lord Jesus' Name. Amen.

Read Matthew 16:16–23.

1. What does Peter do that warrants Jesus' commendation?

_____

_____

_____

_____

2. What does Peter do that warrants Jesus' rebuke?

_____

_____

_____

_____

3. How was Peter's response to Jesus' talk of His death consistent with his understanding of Jesus' identity?

_____

_____

_____

_____

4. Why did Peter question Jesus' description of His impending suffering and death?

_____

_____

_____

_____

5. Why do you think most Christians balk at "suffering and problems"?

_____

_____

_____

_____

6. How do you tend to respond to suffering and problems in your life?

_____

_____

_____

_____

7. Write a definition of "the abundant life" that allows for hardship and hurt yet recognizes that God is in control.

_____

_____

_____

_____

Jesus, Peter got it right and got it wrong on the same day. I can relate. Somehow I've allowed myself to believe that the life You have for me only includes wonderful plans. If God's will for Your life included a cross, should I expect any less? Help me today to expect disappointment and difficulty and to prepare for them with Your Spirit's help. In our Lord Jesus' Name. Amen.

FRIDAY

Read John 13:3–17.

1. What did Jesus do for His disciples as the Last Supper began?

   _____

   _____

   _____

   _____

2. Why did He do that servant's task?

   _____

   _____

   _____

   _____

3. What was Peter's initial reaction when Jesus indicated He wanted to wash his feet?

   _____

   _____

   _____

   _____

4. What was Peter's reaction when he knew that the water stood for spiritual cleansing?

   _____

   _____

   _____

   _____

5. How would you respond if you discovered Jesus kneeling by your feet, preparing to wash them?

   _____

   _____

   _____

   _____

6. Peter's initial resistance was a "pride thing." What is Jesus' attitude toward our pride?

_____
_____
_____
_____

7. If foot washing signifies the grit and grime of daily transgressions, what is something you need to confess to the Lord so that He might "wash your feet"?

_____
_____
_____
_____

∝ *Imitating the Master* ∝

Lord Jesus, thanks for the lessons I'm learning as I look at Peter's life. I'm grateful he is enough like me so that I am not intimidated by his spiritual pedigree. As I picture myself in the Upper Room, I think I would have reacted just like he did when You stooped to wash his feet. Today I feel I have failed You in the area of _____.
Please forgive me. I claim the promise of Your Word that if we confess our sin,
You are faithful and can be depended upon to forgive our sin and cleanse us.
Thanks for doing that. In our Lord Jesus' Name. Amen.

FOR LEADERS

(Notes and suggested answers for selected questions.)

ANOTHER LOOK

1. The fact that Peter's name is the first in all four lists of the Twelve indicates that he stood out as the leader and the spokesman for the whole company of apostles.

2. Whenever Peter is mentioned in a secular context (referring to his house, his mother-in-law, his fishing business, etc.), the Scriptures refer to him by his given name, Simon. The other time he is called by this name is when he is displaying characteristics of his unregenerate self.

3. Apparently John couldn't make up his mind because he saw both sides of Peter constantly.

4. The character qualities that Peter learned were:
   • Submission
   • Restraint
   • Humility
   • Love
   • Compassion
   • Courage

5. When people are following your lead, constantly praising you, looking up to you, and admiring you, it is too easy to be overcome with pride. As a result, pride is a besetting sin of leaders to think of themselves more highly than they should.

BIBLICAL CONNECTIONS

8. Peter denied that he knew Jesus three times (just as Jesus predicted he would). Graciously, Jesus allows Peter the opportunity to affirm his love three times as a way of helping Peter make peace with himself.

10. In 1 Peter 5:8–10, Peter writes to his readers as one who has experienced the paw prints and claw marks of the hungry lion. He has suffered because of poor choices or prideful ambition. But Peter encourages his readers by reminding them that this kind of suffering (as well as being persecuted for one's faith) is part of what it means to live as a Christian in a fallen world. It is to be expected.

HIGHLIGHTING THE LESSON

11. Jesus wanted to remind Peter of his potential as a rock-solid leader. By use of his name, Jesus wanted to challenge Peter's tendencies to be unreliable and shifty.

12. Peter's raw personality consisted of:
    • His inquisitiveness
    • His initiative
    • His involvement

14. Jesus allowed Peter to learn leadership by trial and error. Peter's firsthand experiences gave him empathy and wisdom by which he could model personal and spiritual growth.

DAILY ASSIGNMENTS

Encourage the group participants not only to read the chapter in *Twelve Ordinary Men* assigned for the next lesson (chapter 3), but to use the Daily Assignments to review and remember the truth from God's Word you have just discussed.

4

Andrew: A Brother in the Background

BIBLICAL FOCUS

Key passages from this section of the book: John 1:19–37, 40–42; 6:9–13; 12:20–22; Luke 21:1–4; 1 Corinthians 1:27–29.

READING ASSIGNMENT

Read chapter 3 of *Twelve Ordinary Men.*

ANOTHER LOOK

The following questions will help you review the material you read in the book.

1. MacArthur writes, "Peter and Andrew were originally from the village of Bethsaida (John 1:44)" (pp. 61–62). But that is not where they are living when we meet them in the Gospels. To where have they relocated and what do you know about this place?

   _____

   _____

   _____

   _____

2. According to the author, "Of the four in the inner circle . . . Andrew was the least conspicuous" (p. 63). Why is this true?

   _____

   _____

   _____

   _____

3. What indication is there that Andrew was a devout man before he met Jesus (p. 64)?

   _____

   _____

   _____

   _____

4. Why does the author spend as much time as he does introducing us to a Boston Sunday school teacher by the name of Edward Kimball (p. 69)? How does his life relate to the message of this chapter?

_____

_____

_____

_____

5. MacArthur notes what tradition has to say about Andrew's death (p. 74). How did he supposedly die? What can you glean from this?

_____

_____

_____

_____

> The church I pastor seeks to foster an evangelistic environment. And people are coming to Christ on a regular basis. Almost every Sunday in our evening services we baptize several new believers. Each one gives a testimony before being baptized. And in the overwhelming majority of instances, they tell us they came to Christ primarily because of the testimony of a coworker, a neighbor, a relative, or a friend. Occasionally we hear people say they were converted in direct response to a message they heard in church or a sermon that was broadcast on the radio. But even in those cases, it is usually owing to the influence of an individual who encouraged the person to listen or brought him to church in the first place. There's no question that the most effective means for bringing people to Christ is one at a time, on an individual basis.
>
> —_Twelve Ordinary Men, pp. 68–69_

BIBLICAL CONNECTIONS

These questions will allow you to think through the biblical passages John MacArthur uses in this particular lesson.

6. In the verse that accompanies the title on page 61, we learn that Andrew met Jesus after traveling from his village to hear John the Baptist. But we also learn that Andrew sought out his brother Simon before telling anyone else of his discovery. What does this say about Andrew's relationship with Simon? What does it suggest about reaching family members for Christ?

_____

_____

_____

_____

7. Read John 1:19–37. According to this passage, what prevents someone from reaching the conclusion that Andrew and John were fickle and lacked commitment because of the way they left John the Baptist for Jesus?

_____

_____

_____

_____

8. Contrast John 1:35–37 with Matthew 4:18–22. What about these two passages indicates that, for these four men, following Christ had been a process that involved the passage of time?

_____

_____

_____

_____

9. Now contrast Matthew 4:18–22 with Luke 5:1–11. What obvious omission do you notice? What do you make of that omission?

_____

_____

_____

_____

WORD FOCUS

Andrew's name means "manly," and it seems a fitting description. Of course, the kind of net-fishing he and the others did required no small degree of physical strength and machismo. But Andrew also had other characteristics of manliness. He was bold, decisive, and deliberate. Nothing about him is feeble or wimpish. He was driven by a hearty passion for the truth, and he was willing to subject himself to the most extreme kinds of hardship and austerity in pursuit of that objective.

—*Twelve Ordinary Men, p. 64*

HIGHLIGHTING THE LESSON

These questions have been designed to help you identify the central points MacArthur has made in this section of the book.

10. According to the author, what four indicators can you trace in Scripture that imply that Andrew had the right heart in order to be used effectively in the background (p. 63)?

_____

_____

_____

_____

11. The author characterizes Andrew as the disciple who saw the value of the individual person and, in turn, brought that person to Christ. Other than the fact that he brought his brother to Jesus, what evidence is there in the Gospels for this statement (pp. 67–68)?

_____

_____

_____

_____

12. One day Jesus taught the Twelve about the significance of "insignificant gifts" when he saw a widow placing a couple of coins in the treasury (Luke 21:1–4). Apparently Andrew had already learned this lesson based on a previous incident. What was that incident and how did it reveal something of Andrew's grasp of Jesus' core values?

_____

_____

_____

_____

13. MacArthur writes, "Andrew is the very picture of all those who labor quietly in humble places, 'not with eyeservice, as men-pleasers, but as bondservants of Christ, doing the will of God from the heart' (Ephesians 6:6)" (p. 74). Which of the following organs of the human body do you think matches Andrew's function in the body of disciples? Why?
   • Head
   • Feet
   • Eye
   • Heart
   • Hand

14. Almost from the beginning, the organizers of the Billy Graham Evangelistic Crusades have included a program called "Operation Andrew." It is a people-to-people approach to inviting friends, neighbors, and family members to attend one of the huge rallies. Why do you think it came to be called this? Do you know someone who effectively utilizes this approach in inviting people to your church? Describe that person.

> ℘ Most pastors would love to have their churches populated by people with Andrew's mentality. Too many Christians think that because they can't speak in front of groups or because they don't have leadership gifts, they aren't responsible to evangelize. There are few who, like Andrew, understand the value of befriending just one person and bringing him or her to Christ.
>
> —*Twelve Ordinary Men,* pp. 70

LASTING IMPLICATIONS

The following questions will assist you in drawing personal conclusions from God's Word.

15. Why does the author claim that Andrew is a better model for most church leaders than Peter? Would you say that the most effective leaders in your church resemble Andrew or Peter? Why?

_____

_____

_____

_____

16. MacArthur writes, "Most people do not come to Christ as an immediate response to a sermon they hear in a crowded setting. They come to Christ because of the influence of an individual" (p. 68). Who do you think credits your influence?

_____

_____

_____

_____

17. Looking back, what individual (or individuals) do you credit with inviting you to church or sharing Christ with you?

_____

_____

_____

_____

18. Andrew realized that no gift placed in Jesus' hands was insignificant. If you were to come to that same realization, how would your attitude toward giving to God's work be impacted?

_____

_____

_____

_____

19. In the previous sidebar, MacArthur makes reference to the quiet individuals who labor "faithfully but inconspicuously" yet accomplish the most for the Lord. What does it take to become a person like that? Who in your church would fit that description?

_____

_____

_____

_____

> ℭ Thank God for people like Andrew. They're the quiet indiviauls, laboring faithfully but inconspicuously, giving insignificant, sacrificial gifts, who accomplish the most for the Lord. They don't receive much recognition, but they don't seek it. They only want to hear the Lord say, "Well done."
>
> And Andrew's legacy is the example he left to show us that in effective ministry it's often the little things that count—the individual people, the insignificant gift, and the inconspiuous service. God delights to use such things, because He has "chosen the foolish things of the world to put to shame the wise, and God has chosen the weak things of the world to put to shame the things which are mighty; and the base things of the world and the things which are despised God has chosen, and the things which are not, to bring to nothing the things that are, that no flesh should glory in His presence" (1 Corinthians 1:27–29)
>
> —*Twelve Ordinary Men, p. 75*

DAILY ASSIGNMENTS

MONDAY

Read John 1:35–42.

1. What did Jesus say to Andrew and the others who were following Him?

    _____

    _____

    _____

    _____

2. What did they say to Him?

    _____

    _____

    _____

    _____

3. What is implied by the reference to the time of day John includes in this description?

    _____

    _____

    _____

    _____

4. How much time do you think they spent in conversation with Jesus at the place where He was lodging?

5. In what sense does Jesus still invite those who follow Him to "come and see"?

6. How much time does it take for you to adequately hear from the Lord each day through Bible study and prayer?

7. What action could you take to move you in the direction of spending the kind of time you just described as adequate for attentive listening to the Lord?

Lord, it is obvious that Andrew had a curious heart. He was not content to simply be a fisherman. He followed John and then he followed You. He wanted to know where You were staying. In all honesty, Jesus, I am too preoccupied with my agenda to spend the kind of time seeking You that I should. Today I want to pause and listen for Your voice inviting me to "come and see" what You have for me.
In our Lord Jesus' Name. Amen.

1. How does Matthew describe John the Baptist?

NOTES

2. Why was John the Baptist such a phenomenon?

_____

_____

_____

_____

3. Since Andrew had become a follower of John the Baptist, is it safe to say that he was willing to embrace the elements of such an austere lifestyle? Why or why not?

_____

_____

_____

_____

4. Andrew's name means "manly." Based on what you know of his temperament, does he live up to his name? Explain.

_____

_____

_____

_____

5. Whereas Peter was more of a driven personality, Andrew was much more laid back. Which of these two men do you tend to resemble?

_____

_____

_____

_____

6. Would you say that your similarity to Peter or Andrew involves aspects that God primarily uses to work _in_ you (such as Peter's impulsiveness leading to training in forethought) or that God uses to work _through_ you (such as Andrew's ability to draw others into the circle)?

_____

_____

_____

_____

7. Andrew's decision to follow John the Baptist before he followed Jesus indicates a willingness to commit to a cause beyond his fishing business. What cause(s) would people who know you say you are captivated by?

_____

_____

_____

_____

Jesus, You know what I value most. Although I am making progress in prioritizing my walk with You, I have a long way to go. Too often I take my cues from a culture that hints at what a real man or a worldly-wise woman should be like. Help me draw from Andrew's example a decidedly different standard. Open my eyes to his willingness to commit to a cause that wasn't all that popular.
In our Lord Jesus' Name. Amen.

WEDNESDAY

Read Matthew 4:18–22.

1. Why were Andrew and Peter fishing?

2. This event takes place some time following Andrew's first encounter with Jesus. What else is different about this scene from the one in the first chapter of John's Gospel?

3. How significant is the word "immediately"?

4. Write out at least two sentences that use the word "immediately" to describe decisions you made or actions you took based on God's Word.

5. When have you found yourself verbalizing your desire to spend more time with the Lord? When have you sensed the Lord calling you to lay down your work and spend time with Him?

6. For Andrew and the other three fisherman "following Jesus" meant exactly that-physical following. What does it mean today when Jesus commands someone to "follow" Him?

_____

_____

_____

_____

7. How would you describe the status of your relationship with Jesus when it comes to the matter of following Him?

_____

_____

_____

_____

∂ *Imitating the Master* ∂

You've called me to follow You, Lord. I am impressed by how Andrew and Peter
immediately heeded Your call. Yet they still had a lot to learn about
what it meant to truly "follow" You each day. Help me to
willingly follow You each day, Lord. In our Lord Jesus' Name. Amen.

THURSDAY

Read John 6:8–13.

1. What fact did Andrew bring to Jesus' attention?

_____

_____

_____

_____

2. Why was Andrew attuned to the young boy and his lunch?

_____

_____

_____

_____

3. How much food was left over after the multitude of thousands was fed?

_____

_____

_____

_____

4. What aspect of this miracle intrigues you the most? What part would you most like to watch on "instant replay"?

_____

_____

_____

_____

5. In what way is this picture of exponential increase similar to the story of D. L. Moody that MacArthur tells in this chapter (pp. 69–70)?

_____

_____

_____

_____

6. Describe a time in your church when a seemingly insignificant action paved the way for a major accomplishment or blessing to many.

_____

_____

_____

_____

7. When was the last time God used something "little" that you did to surprise you with greater results than you imagined?

_____

_____

_____

_____

❧ Imitating the Master ❧

Jesus, I'm inspired by the reality of what really happened on the hillside near the Sea of Galilee so long ago. Andrew introduced a little boy to You, and You accomplished what no one thought possible. Please sensitize me to the "insignificant people" in my sphere of influence who might very well be the means You'd use to accomplish something great in our community or church. In our Lord Jesus' Name. Amen.

FRIDAY

Read Mark 9:33–37.

1. Why did the disciples hesitate to tell Jesus what they had been discussing on the road?

_____

_____

_____

_____

2. How did Jesus' definition of greatness differ from that of the disciples?

_____

_____

_____

_____

3. Jesus actually used two unexpected illustrations to explain His standard of greatness. What were they?

_____

_____

_____

_____

4 . Does Andrew conjure up this kind of person in your mind? Why or why not?

_____

_____

_____

_____

5. Jesus' job description for greatness is one that He Himself followed (see Mark 10:43–45). In contrast to a call to merely walk behind Him, what does Jesus mean when He says, "Follow Me"?

_____

_____

_____

_____

6. What is it about "servanthood" that is hard to swallow for most people?

_____

_____

_____

_____

7. If you were to give the "Andrew of the Year" award to someone in your congregation, who would that be? Why?

_____

_____

_____

_____

Lord Jesus, when I think of Andrew, I think of _____ in our church. That person is so willing to be used by You and yet so willing to be in the background. I want to learn from his/her example. Forgive me for all the times when I try to steal the limelight or insist on having things my way. Will You start today, Jesus, by prompting me to look for someone whom I might serve with some secret act of Christian love? In our Lord Jesus' Name. Amen.

FOR LEADERS

(Notes and suggested answers for selected questions.)

ANOTHER LOOK

1. They have relocated to Capernaum. Although near to their hometown of Bethsaida, it was an especially advantageous location for their fishing business. Capernaum was located on the north shore of the Sea of Galilee (where fishing was good) and at the junction of the key trade routes.

2. Scripture doesn't tell us a lot about him. There are limited references to Andrew in the Gospels. Only nine times (apart from the group listings of the disciples) is Andrew mentioned, and most of these references are insignificant ones.

3. He traveled some distance from Capernaum to hear John the Baptist preach in the Judean wilderness.

4. Edward Kimball, like Andrew, was not an up-front leader type. But he did make a significant contribution to church history by introducing young Dwight Moody to Christ. Moody in turn influenced millions for the kingdom of God. That is in essence what Andrew did when he brought Peter to Jesus. Without Andrew or Mr. Kimball, those in the spotlight might never have gotten there.

5. He was lashed to an x-shaped cross instead of being nailed to one. That way he suffered longer. Still, as he hung on a cross for two days, tradition records that Andrew exhorted passersby to confess faith in Jesus.

BIBLICAL CONNECTIONS

6. When someone comes to faith in Christ, the most natural response is to want to share the joy of salvation with those to whom he or she is closest.

7. No, they were not fickle. John the Baptist had already admitted that he wasn't the ultimate goal of their search. In fact, he pointed them to the One who was. This was John's way of releasing his new disciples to become disciples of Jesus.

8. The two sets of brothers had returned to their fishing business in Capernaum after their first encounter with Jesus in Judea. It's conceivable that several months could have passed.

9. Andrew's name is missing from Luke's account. This is one of the indicators that Andrew was in the background much of the time and (according to MacArthur) accepted that behind-the-scenes role.

HIGHLIGHTING THE LESSON

10. The indicators that Andrew had a right heart are as follows:
    - He did not seek to be the center of attention.
    - Of the "inner circle of disciples," Andrew was the most thoughtful.
    - Whenever he acted by himself, he did what was right.
    - Whenever his name is expressly mentioned, Scripture commends him.

11. On the day Jesus wanted to feed the multitude, Andrew was aware of the boy who had the loaves and fish. When a small group of Greek seekers approached Philip asking to see Jesus, he approached Andrew in order to expedite their request.

12. In John 6, Andrew spotted the boy with the fish and bread in the crowd. Even though he knew that it would not feed the multitude "as is," he saw the boy's lunch as something Jesus could use.

DAILY ASSIGNMENTS

Encourage the group participants not only to read the chapter in *Twelve Ordinary Men* assigned for the next lesson (chapter 4), but to use the Daily Assignments to review and remember the truth from God's Word you have just discussed.

5

James: One Son of Thunder

BIBLICAL FOCUS

Key passages from this section of the book: 2 Kings 1:3–17; Ecclesiastes 3:1–8; Matthew 17:1; 20:20–24; Mark 5:37; 13:3; 14:33; Luke 9:51–56; Acts 12:1–3.

READING ASSIGNMENT

Read chapter 4 of *Twelve Ordinary Men.*

ANOTHER LOOK

The following questions will help you review the material you read in the book.

1. MacArthur describes Zebedee, the father of James and John, as a man of importance. In addition to having a fishing business large enough to employ multiple people, what would lead him to think that?

   _____
   _____
   _____
   _____

2. According to the author, "James is a much more significant figure than we might consider, based on the little we know about him. . . . There is good reason to assume he was a strong leader . . . [He] also figures prominently in the close inner circle of three" (p. 78). What four evidences does the author give?

   _____
   _____
   _____
   _____

3. What is the reason MacArthur suggests that James was the first of the Twelve to be martyred?

   _____
   _____
   _____
   _____

4. Describe how the mixed-race group of people known as Samaritans came about.

_____

_____

_____

_____

5. The author categorically states that the reason the Samaritans rejected Jesus' request for accommodations had nothing to do with a lack of vacancy in the city's inns. What was the reason He and His disciples were turned away?

_____

_____

_____

_____

> ℰ Mark, who records that Jesus called James and John "Sons of Thunder," includes that fact in his list of the Twelve, mentioning it in the same way he notes that Simon was named Peter (Mark 3:17). We don't know how often Jesus employed His nickname for James and John; Mark's mention of it is the only time it appears in all of Scripture. Unlike Peter's name, which was obviously intended to help encourage and shape Peter's character toward a rocklike steadfastness, *Boanerges* seems to have been bestowed on the sons of Zebedee to chide them when they allowed their naturally feverish temperaments to get out of hand. Perhaps the Lord even used it for humorous effect while employing it as a gentle admonishment.
>
> —*Twelve Ordinary Men, pp. 79–80*

BIBLICAL CONNECTIONS

These questions will allow you to think through the biblical passages John MacArthur uses in this particular lesson.

6. In 2 Kings 9:20–10:31, we are introduced to one of Israel's more colorful kings. After reading this passage and based on what you know about James, compare their similarities and differences.

_____

_____

_____

_____

7. Zeal can be a quality of one who is spiritually mature. But that is not always the case. Zeal is the root of the word "zealots," people who were known to kill to achieve their political ends. What differences do you detect in the

zealousness for God as seen in John 2:17 and Romans 10:2? What appears to be the determining factor that makes for godly zeal?

_____

_____

_____

_____

8. James and John's inclination to call down fire from heaven on the inhospitable Samaritans was not original with them. It was based on an experience Elijah had in this same region several centuries before. Read 2 Kings 1:3–17. Why was it appropriate for Elijah to invoke divine judgment, but inappropriate for James and John to do so?

_____

_____

_____

_____

9. No doubt James and John were clueless as to why they were not permitted to play the judgment card in response to the way the Samaritans dealt with Jesus and the Twelve. It would become clearer once they understood "the rest of the story." You can find that in Acts 8:5–8. Which of the following headlines best captures what this entire story was about? Why? (Circle one and then explain using the blanks below).
   • FORECASTED FIRESTORM FAILS TO DEVELOP
   • SAMARITANS CHANGE THEIR MINDS ABOUT MESSIAH
   • UNEXPECTED INVESTMENT IN PEACE PAYS BIG DIVIDENDS
   • FLAMES OF JUDGMENT GIVE WAY TO PENTECOSTAL FIRE
   • SCOLDED DISCIPLES DENOUNCE PHILIP THE EVANGELIST

_____

_____

_____

_____

10. One of the reasons Jesus didn't allow James and his brother to call down fire was His reluctance to use the supernatural to establish His agenda (see Matthew 12:39). But even more significant was the approach Jesus took toward those who opposed Him. What stands out in each of the following passages that gives insight into Jesus' purpose at His first coming?
   • Luke 19:10
   • Matthew 20:28
   • John 3:16–17
   • Luke 9:55–56
   • John 12:46–47

_____

_____

_____

WORD FOCUS

Inquiring of soothsayers was strictly forbidden by Moses' law, of course (Deuteronomy 18:10-12). Seeking prophecies from fortune-tellers who were associated with Baal-Zebub was even worse. Baal-Zebub was a Philistine deity. His name meant "lord of the flies." The land of the Philistines was thick with flies, and the Philistines believed the lord of the flies lived in their land, so they made this fly-god one of their main deities. They had some famous oracles who claimed to be able to tell the future. They usually gave flattering prophecies with predictions so ambiguous they could hardly miss, but those oracles nonetheless had gained famed throughout Israel. They were the "Psychic Friends Network" of Elijah's time.

But Baal-Zebub was as vile a deity as anyone ever invented. He supposedly ruled the flies—those abhorrent insects that swarm around every kind of decay and filth and spread disease and spawn maggots. It was a fitting image for this kind of god. Who would ever think of worshiping a deity whose realm was everything foul and unclean? Such a god was so revolting to the Jews that they altered the name *Baal-Zebub* slightly to make it "Beelzebul," which means "god of dung." This vile being epitomized everything impure and unholy—everything that opposes the true God. (That is why, by the time of Jesus, the name *Beelzebub* had become a way to refer to Satan—Luke 11:15.) This was the god from whom Ahaziah sought knowledge of the future.

—Twelve Ordinary Men, pp. 84–85

HIGHLIGHTING THE LESSON

These questions have been designed to help you identify the central points MacArthur has made in this section of the book.

11. The Scriptures picture James as someone with a thunderous personality. Is that quality necessarily bad? For the following personalities, was that a positive or a negative trait?

    • Elijah

    • Nehemiah

    • John the Baptist

    • Jesus

12. James obviously was familiar with the Old Testament account of Elijah calling down fire on the emissaries of Ahaziah. He knew the Scriptures, but the manner in which he let the Lord know what was on his (and his brother's) mind was not scripturally sound. What was only too apparent in his words,

"Lord, do You want us to command fire to come down from heaven and consume them" (Luke 9:54)?

_____

_____

_____

_____

13. Besides being fervent, passionate, zealous, and insensitive, James was also ambitious and overconfident. He wanted to gain status over the other disciples. It seems that he was able to persuade his mother to approach Jesus to ask that he and his brother John be given preferential treatment. Knowing what you know about James, does that surprise you? Are these leadership qualities neutral, negative, or positive? Explain.

_____

_____

_____

_____

14. James was the first disciple to lose his life (other than Judas who took his own life). As has been expressed previously, Herod's decision to go after James no doubt had to do with James's personality. But what do you gather from the fact that James did not run away from the contract put out on his life?

_____

_____

_____

_____

LASTING IMPLICATIONS

The following questions will assist you in drawing personal conclusions from God's Word.

15. Knowing James had grown up in a well-to-do home (perhaps with feelings of "entitlement") makes it easier to understand why he was one of those involved in debates over who deserved to be considered "the greatest" of the disciples. How has your family of origin influenced the kinds of things you expect of God?

_____

_____

_____

_____

16. According to MacArthur, "The Samaritans' religion is a classic example of what happens when the authority of Scripture is subjugated to human tradition" (p. 82). Which of the following are contemporary examples of that phenomenon?
- Doing penance in exchange for having a confessed sin forgiven.

- Making weekly worship as a family a priority.

- Forbidding the use of alcohol and tobacco.

- Accommodating the practice of homosexuality as an acceptable lifestyle for Christians.

- Giving generously to the Lord's work in proportion to His blessings.

17. James and John's desire to call down fire indicates that it is indeed possible to sound religious but have wrong motives. When do you think people are most tempted to cover their wrong motives by quoting a verse or example from the Bible?

_____
_____
_____
_____

18. Do you concur with what the author says about someone who is passionate and enthusiastic (but with a potential for failure) being more desirable than "a cold compromiser" (p. 94)? Why or why not?

_____
_____
_____
_____

19. Can you identify someone who has influenced your life for Christ in a positive way—someone who reminds you of James? If so, how did that person shape your Christian devotion?

_____
_____
_____
_____

> James wanted a crown of glory; Jesus gave him a cup of suffering. He wanted power; Jesus gave him servanthood. He wanted a place of prominence; Jesus gave him a martyr's grave. He wanted to rule; Jesus gave him a sword—not to wield, but to be the instrument of his own execution. Fourteen years after this, James would become the first of the Twelve to be killed for his faith.
>
> —*Twelve Ordinary Men, p. 91*

DAILY ASSIGNMENTS

MONDAY

Read Matthew 17:1; Mark 5:37; 13:3; 14:33.

1. List the people who are present in each scene.

    _____
    _____
    _____
    _____

2. Briefly describe each situation:
    *   Matthew 17:1—

    *   Mark 5:37—

    *   Mark 13:3—

    *   Mark 14:33—

3. In which passage did James experience the following:
    *   Jesus' agony

    *   Jesus' sovereignty

    *   Jesus' power

    *   Jesus' glory

4. How would his firsthand experience of these events have impacted James's faith?

    _____
    _____
    _____
    _____

5. If you had been a witness to these events, how do you think it would have affected your faith?

    _____
    _____
    _____
    _____

6. Which of the four experiences of Jesus' identity do you think prepared James for the martyrdom he would eventually face? Why?

    _____
    _____

_____

_____

7. Which of the four evidences of Jesus' uniqueness listed above have made the deepest impact on your own life?

_____

_____

_____

_____

♫ *Imitating the Master* ♫

Lord, as I read passages like the ones I read today, I wish I could have been there with You as You touched people's lives and demonstrated God's power. Help me to sense Your presence and power as I read Your Word each day.
In our Lord Jesus' Name. Amen.

TUESDAY

Read Luke 9:51–56.

1. What prompted James and John to suggest calling down fire on the Samaritans?

_____

_____

_____

_____

2. What personal attitudes are revealed by their response?

_____

_____

_____

_____

3. When Jesus refused their suggestion, what response to the lodging dilemma did He propose?

_____

_____

_____

_____

4. What in the two brothers' response to the Samaritans' denial of accommodations strikes you as arrogant?

_____

_____

_____

5. Describe a situation you know of where Christians have acted in a condescending manner toward those who are obviously ungodly.

_____

_____

_____

_____

6. How would Jesus respond to such super-spirituality?

_____

_____

_____

_____

7. What have you learned about yourself from your reading today?

_____

_____

_____

_____

❧ *Imitating the Master* ❧

Jesus, as I go about my daily routines today, there no doubt will be times when I want to strike out at others instead of seeking a peaceful solution. Help me respond patiently and with understanding to people who don't know You.
In our Lord Jesus' Name. Amen.

WEDNESDAY

Read Ecclesiastes 3:1–8.

1. What kinds of life situations does this passage deal with?

_____

_____

_____

_____

2. What seems to be the bottom-line message of this poem?

_____

_____

_____

_____

3. As far as Jesus was concerned, the lack of hospitality in Samaria was not a time to kill. Using the words or phrases in this passage, what time did Jesus imply that it was?

_____

_____
_____
_____
_____

4. James must have felt reprimanded when Jesus refused his suggestion. How was this a growing experience for this passionate disciple?

_____
_____
_____
_____

5. Timing is everything. What is right sometimes is wrong other times. How do you determine how God wants you to act at any given time?

_____
_____
_____
_____

6. Describe an occasion in your life when your first reaction turned out to be wrong but led to your discovering some important lessons about responding in Christ's way?

_____
_____
_____
_____

7. Referring back to that list in Ecclesiastes, how would you describe the times in your life right now?

_____
_____
_____
_____

❧ Imitating the Master ❧

You know my tendencies, Lord. I am not always good at discerning what You want me to do. King Solomon's poetry is worth pondering. I want to respond to the situations You bring into my life appropriately. Give me the wisdom to know the "times and seasons" in my world so that I can act in a way that pleases You and benefits others. In our Lord Jesus' name. Amen.

THURSDAY

Read Matthew 20:20–24.

1. Identify the cast of characters in this one-act play.

_____

_____

_____

_____

_____

2   How does Jesus respond to James's mother's request?

_____

_____

_____

_____

3. What exactly did Jesus grant and what did He withhold in His response to James's mother?

_____

_____

_____

_____

4. What about this scene is consistent with the fact that Zebedee was a man of wealth and influence?

_____

_____

_____

_____

5. Does it strike you as disingenuous when James and John quickly agree that they can drink the cup of sorrow? Why or why not?

_____

_____

_____

_____

6. The other ten were put off by James and John's mother's request of Jesus. Do you think they were upset that their moms had not beat her to the punch? Or do you think they were above such pettiness? Explain.

_____

_____

_____

_____

7. When you consider the behavior of the Twelve on this particular occasion, what attitudes does it remind you to be cautious about?

_____

_____

_____

_____

Jesus, I'm not sure my mother would have tried to push me to the front of the pack.
But when I'm honest with myself, I have to admit that I have those tendencies.
I want what is best for me. I want to look good. I want to make sure
I've covered my options. Me. Me. Me. Help me today, Lord,
to forget about me and focus on You. In our Lord Jesus' Name. Amen.

FRIDAY

Read Luke 22:24–34.

1. What ungodly behavior in this passage is not attributed to individuals by name? Which one is tied to an individual?

     _____
     _____
     _____
     _____

2. How does Peter's failure illustrate how easy it is to perceive greatness in oneself that is not merited?

     _____
     _____
     _____
     _____

3. Why did Jesus take time to tell Peter the extent of his future failure? (Refer to John 21:15–22.)

     _____
     _____
     _____
     _____

4. If other disciples had joined the debate of "who's the greatest," it only reveals that the propensity to position oneself above others is not limited to the wealthy. Why do you think people who lack material possessions are tempted by the same things as those who "have it all"?

     _____
     _____
     _____
     _____

5. As you consider Christians in your sphere of influence, which temptation is more difficult to resist: issues of personal status (like the disciples at large), or being embarrassed of Christ when scrutinized for their faith (like Peter)?

     _____
     _____

6. Ironically, the debate over "who's the best" occurred at the Last Supper. Try to identify a time in your life when you have been surrounded by Christian influences and input only to give in to ungodly thoughts or actions.

_____

_____

_____

_____

7. Revisit John 21:15–22. How often do you sense that Jesus needs to have the kind of conversation with you that He had with Peter?

_____

_____

_____

_____

♂ *Imitating the Master* ♂

Lord Jesus, the world in which I live is filled with all kinds of temptations. James dealt with issues of pride and selfishness. Peter dealt with issues of honesty and denial. I know what my signature sins are. I ask for Your help as I deal with _____. In our Lord Jesus' Name. Amen.

FOR LEADERS

(Notes and suggested answers for selected questions.)

ANOTHER LOOK

1. Zebedee must have had status for his son John to have been known to the high priest, which is how John was able to get Peter admitted to the high priest's courtyard on the night of Jesus' arrest (see John 18:15–16). There is also evidence from an early church record that Zebedee was a Levite and closely related to the high priest's family. In addition to this, when Matthew introduces us to James and John, he simply refers to them as the sons of Zebedee (as if his readers would have known who that was).

2. Here are the times we see James in the inner circle:
   - Only he, Peter, and John were permitted to go with Jesus when He raised Jairus's daughter from the dead (Mark 5:37).
   - The same group of three witnessed Jesus' glory on the Mount of Transfiguration (Matthew 17:1).

- He was among the four who questioned Jesus privately on the Mount of Olives (Mark 13:3).
- He was included again with Peter and John when the Lord urged these three to pray with Him privately in Gethsemane (Mark 14:33).

3. It no doubt had to do with the fact that he was not a passive or subtle man, but was rather the kind of person who stirred things up, making great enemies rapidly.

4. The Samaritans were the offspring of Israelites from the Northern Kingdom who intermarried and had children with the Assyrians who had conquered their land.

5. Jesus was on His way to worship in Jerusalem. This angered the Samaritans since they believed that the only true place to worship God was in their area on Mount Gerizim. Because they knew Jesus' intentions, they denied His request.

BIBLICAL CONNECTIONS

6. Jehu had a similar personality to James. Both were men of intense fervor and passion. James, however, had a heart to please God, whereas Jehu's zeal for the Lord was tainted with selfish ambition.

7. Zeal that is based on personal ambition is misguided passion. That which is grounded in the knowledge of God's will and Word is legitimate.

8. Elijah's mission was much different from Jesus' mission. At the time in which he lived, Elijah's role as a prophet was to mete out judgment against extreme wickedness and to maintain God's glory. At this first coming, Jesus was revealing a different perspective of God's agenda.

10. The answers are as follows:
- Luke 19:10, "The Son of Man has come to seek and to save that which was lost."
- Matthew 20:28, "The Son of Man did not come to be served, but to serve, and to give His life a ransom for many."
- John 3:16–17, "For God so loved the world that He gave His only begotten Son, that whoever believes in Him should not perish but have everlasting life. For God did not send His Son into the world to condemn the world, but that the world through Him might be saved."
- Luke 9:55–56, "The Son of Man did not come to destroy men's lives but to save them."
- John 12:46–47, "I have come as a light into the world, that whoever believes in Me should not abide in darkness. And if anyone hears My words and does not believe, I do not judge him; for I did not come to judge the world but to save the world."

11. In all four cases it was a positive trait. They were zealous for the right reasons.

12. James and John may have been interested in defending Jesus' rights and privileges as Messiah, but their motives were all wrong. The tone of their question smacks of arrogance.

DAILY ASSIGNMENTS

Encourage the group participants not only to read the chapter in *Twelve Ordinary Men* assigned for the next lesson (chapter 5), but to use the Daily Assignments to review and remember the truth from God's Word you have just discussed.

6

John: A Study in Transformation

BIBLICAL FOCUS

Key passages from this section of the book: Mark 9:1–41; Ephesians 4:13–15.

READING ASSIGNMENT

Read chapter 5 of *Twelve Ordinary Men.*

ANOTHER LOOK

The following questions will help you review the material you read in the book.

1. MacArthur joins other biblical scholars who recognize how remarkable it is
    that one of the "Sons of Thunder" earned the nickname "the apostle of
    love" before he died. What three areas of love does the author indicate John
    wrote extensively about?

    _____

    _____

    _____

    _____

2. According to the author, John was not just preoccupied with love. He had
    such a zeal for the truth that it shaped the way he wrote. MacArthur writes,
    "Of all the writers in the New Testament, he is the most black and white in
    his thinking" (p. 97). What examples does MacArthur point out?

    _____

    _____

    _____

> ✎ The theme of love flows through his writings. But love was a
> quality he learned from Christ, not something that came naturally to
> him. In his younger years, he was as much a Son of Thunder as James. If
> you imagine that John was the way he is often portrayed in medieval
> art—a meek, mild, pale-skinned, effeminate person, lying around on
> Jesus' shoulder looking up at Him with a dove-eyed stare—forget that
> caricature. He was rugged and hard-edged, just like the rest of the fisher-
> men disciples. And again, he was every bit as intolerant, ambitious, zeal-
> ous, and explosive as his elder brother.
>
> *—Twelve Ordinary Men, pp. 68*

3. MacArthur's description of John in the sidebar above references John's pre-occupation with love but also his natural tendencies that were more akin to those who shared his occupation as a fisherman. How does the author explain the change that occurred in John?

_____
_____
_____
_____

4. Which one of John's three epistles does the author offer as an example that John finally learned the balance of truth and love?

_____
_____
_____
_____

5. To Peter Jesus said, "Feed my sheep!" What injunction did the dying Savior give to John? What reason does MacArthur offer that Jesus chose John for this task?

_____
_____
_____
_____

BIBLICAL CONNECTIONS

These questions will allow you to think through the biblical passages John MacArthur uses in this particular lesson.

6. Although a hurried reading of John's Gospel would lead one to believe that he doesn't think Christians are capable of sinning, such is not the case. Read 1 John 1:8–2:1. Still, John is not nearly as expressive as Paul when it comes to describing the extent to which believers struggle with sin. Read Romans 7:14–24. Explain why this is.

_____
_____
_____
_____

7. Refresh yourself with the story of Christ's Transfiguration and the events that immediately follow it by reading Mark 9:1-38. Why do the events on the mountain fulfill the prediction Jesus made in verse 1?

_____
_____
_____
_____

8. Since John and his brother James were known by their ambitious natures, why would it be especially difficult for them to obey Jesus and not to talk about their experience on the mountaintop? Why would such a supernatural experience make it especially easy to start debating issues of status?

_____

_____

_____

_____

9. In 1 John 1:9, John celebrates the gift of forgiveness that believers are offered when they come clean and confess their sin. It appears that Jesus helped John discover the discipline of confession years earlier. In the following two episodes in John's relationship with Jesus, MacArthur says confession was involved. Read the verses and describe how confession occurs in each instance.

- Mark 9:33

- Mark 9:35–37

10. In Ephesians 4:13–15, the apostle Paul paints a word picture that portrays spiritual maturity that balances truth with love. As you read these verses, ask yourself, "What about this portrait of maturity suggests that this is a lifetime process?" Do you suspect it was also a lifetime process for John? Why or why not?

_____

_____

_____

_____

 WORD FOCUS

John's love of truth is evident in all his writings. He uses the Greek word for truth twenty-five times in his Gospel and twenty more times in his epistles. He wrote, "I have no greater joy than to hear that my children walk in truth" (3 John 4). His strongest epithet for someone who claimed to be a believer while walking in darkness was to describe the person as "a liar, and the truth is not in him" (1 John 2:4; cf. 1: 6, 8). No one in all Scripture, except the Lord Himself, had more to say extolling the very concept of truth . . .

But it is interesting that he also used the word love more than eighty times. Clearly, he learned the balance Christ taught him. He learned to love others as the Lord had loved him. Love became the anchor and centerpiece of the truth he was most concerned with.

—*Twelve Ordinary Men, pp. 101, 116*

HIGHLIGHTING THE LESSON

These questions have been designed to help you identify the central points MacArthur has made in this section of the book.

11. John, like Andrew, was not a fisherman preoccupied solely with sole. He obviously was a seeker of truth. He traveled far to follow after the austere baptizing prophet. Then he left John the Baptist when he realized Jesus was the Lamb of God. But in spite of John's disciplined search for truth, why was he a difficult person to be around?

   _____

   _____

   _____

   _____

12. In addition to John's low aptitude for tolerance, it appears that John also didn't score too well when it came to humility. Based on what you read in Mark 9 and 10, what leads you to believe that Jesus had a remedial student on His hands in John?

   _____

   _____

   _____

   _____

13. In Mark 9:35–37, Jesus brings a child into the room to help His disciples visualize that growing up spiritually means embracing virtues found in children. Curiously, when John is old and writing epistles, his favorite term for his readers is "my little children." Was this an indication that he finally caught on to what Jesus was trying to get across? Why or why not?

   _____

   _____

   _____

   _____

14. Which of the following indicators of John's growth in humility strikes you as being the most amazing? Why? Circle one and explain your answer in the space provided below.
   • In his Gospel, he never once mentions his own name.
   • He never paints himself in the foreground as a hero.
   • John's Gospel is the only one of the four that details the scene in which Jesus demonstrates humble servanthood by washing His disciples' feet.
   • In his epistles, in addition to calling his readers "little children," he also refers to them as "beloved" and calls himself a brother and a fellow child of God.
   • In Revelation, he refers to himself as a brother and companion even though he is the last surviving apostle.

   _____

   _____

15. Although John mastered his graduate course in learning how to balance truth with love, it appears that suffering was one of the prerequisites for getting a passing grade. What suffering, in addition to bearing the grief of his older brother James's martyrdom, did John have to endure?

_____

_____

_____

_____

> ℰ It is probably fair to say that one of the dangerous tendencies for a man with John's personality is that he would have a natural inclination to push things to extremes. And indeed, it does seem that John in his younger years was a bit of an extremist. He seemed to lack a sense of spiritual equilibrium. His zeal, his sectarianism, his intolerance, and his selfish ambition were all sins of *imbalance*. They were all potential virtues, pushed to sinful extremes. That is why the greatest strengths of his character sometimes ironically *caused* his most prominent failures. Peter and James had a similar tendency to turn their greatest strengths into weaknesses. Their *best* characteristics frequently became pitfalls for them.
> —*Twelve Ordinary Men, p. 99*

LASTING IMPLICATIONS

The following questions will assist you in drawing personal application from God's Word.

16. The young John is remarkably different from the one we meet at the end of our Bibles. He is truly an example of what happens when believers grow in Christ and allow His strength to be made perfect in their weaknesses. What kinds of qualities do you ordinarily associate with someone who is spiritually mature?

_____

_____

_____

_____

17. MacArthur says one of the consequences of our human depravity is that our best characteristics can become an occasion for stumbling. For example, if ambition (a legitimate quality) is not balanced with humility, it becomes sinful pride. How might each of the following good qualities become personally destructive if corrupted by sin?
   * Dedication on the job
   * Financial generosity at church
   * Sensitivity to the feelings of others

18. What is the risk of preaching on love and tolerance to the exclusion of issues that God's Word speaks definitively against? Describe a church you've heard about that was guilty of this extreme.

_____

_____

_____

_____

19. What qualities of children do you think Jesus had in mind when He called the Twelve (and John in particular) to become more like them?

_____

_____

_____

_____

John's theology is best described as a theology of love. He taught that God is a God of love, that God loved His own Son, that God loved the world, that God is loved by Christ, that Christ loved His disciples, that Christ's disciples loved Him, that all men should love Christ, that we should love one another, and that love fulfills the law. Love was critical part of every element of John's teaching. It was the dominant theme of his theology.

And yet his love never slid into tolerant sentimentality. To the very end of his life John was still a thunderous defender of the truth. He lost none of his intolerance for lies. In his epistles, written near the end of his life, he was still thundering out against errant Christologies, against anti-Christian deceptions, against sin, and against immorality. He was in that sense a Son of Thunder to the end. I think the Lord knew that the most powerful advocate of love needed to be a man who never compromised the truth.

—Twelve Ordinary Men, p. 116

DAILY ASSIGNMENTS

MONDAY

Read Mark 9:38–41.

1. What did John confess that he had done?

_____

_____

_____

_____

2. How did Jesus respond?

_____

_____

_____

_____

3. If this were the first exposure you had to John, what kind of a person would you think he was?

_____

_____

_____

_____

4. When you are most inclined to be protective of "your group's ways of doing things"?

_____

_____

_____

_____

5. Which of the following describes how your church welcomes new people?
   • Are you sure we're the church you're looking for?
   • What took you so long? We've been waiting for you!
   • Follow me, I'll show you around.
   • You're new? I didn't know.
   • We're excited about the new ideas you'll bring to our church.

6. What does the answer you chose above say about your church's attitude toward visitors?

_____

_____

_____

_____

7. Which of those five statements do you think most closely expresses the attitude Jesus described to John in the passage above?

_____

_____

_____

_____

∂ *Imitating the Master* ∂

Lord, I pray that our church will be a welcoming place for people. Help me to be a person who is eager to introduce myself and make people feel welcome. Thank You for Your family that draws in so many different kinds of people who can serve You.
In our Lord Jesus' Name. Amen.

TUESDAY

Read Romans 6:6–7.

1. How does Paul describe the Christian's relationship with sin?

_____

_____

_____

_____

2. Now read Romans 7:14–24. Is this a description of someone who is a slave to sin? Why or why not?

_____

_____

_____

_____

3. Paul emphasizes our tendency to fail while John emphasizes our responsibility to live righteously. At what points in your life have you been impacted by what each of those contributors to God's Word has to say?

_____

_____

_____

_____

4. As a way of understanding the ongoing nature of a Christian's warfare with sin, read Hebrews 12:1–2 and write out a description of an ensnaring sin.

_____

_____

_____

_____

5. Based on those you know best at your church, what ensnaring sin seems to be a prevalent one that several are battling?

_____

_____

_____

_____

6. You know what your ensnaring sin is. Based on 1 John 1:9, what advice would John give you?

_____

_____

_____

_____

7. Based on that same verse from 1 John, what can you expect to be God's response to your confession?

_____

_____

_____

_____

✑ *Imitating the Master* ✑

Jesus, I want to thank You for the gift of confession and the corresponding gift of forgiveness. It is so freeing to be able to admit my imperfection and frailty. Thank You for cleansing me. Although I know I'm no longer a slave to sin, I know I still need You to remind me on a daily basis that I belong to You.
In our Lord Jesus' Name. Amen.

WEDNESDAY

Read 1 Corinthians 13:4–5.

1. Paraphrase Paul's words using your own expressions and understanding of his terms.

_____

_____

_____

_____

2. Why would someone like John, who came from a prominent wealthy family, have difficulty digesting this definition of love?

_____

_____

_____

_____

3. Which of the characteristics of God's kind of love do you find most lacking in your life?

_____

_____

_____

_____

4. Which of the characteristics of God's kind of love have you found He is building into your life?

_____

_____

_____

_____

5. When Jesus asked John to care for His mother, Mary, He assigned him homework that would test his love quotient. In what other ways did the Lord test John?

_____

_____

_____

_____

6. When are you most in need of being reminded that loving means giving up your rights?

_____

_____

_____

_____

7. Even though Paul is credited with writing the "love chapter" of the Bible (1 Corinthians 13), John mentions love more than any other New Testament writer. What verse about love in one of John's writings is most familiar to you?

_____

_____

_____

_____

❧ *Imitating the Master* ❧

Lord, I'm grateful for the people You have placed in my life who challenge me to love with my life instead of with my lips alone. Thank You for those around me who really have learned the art of embracing Your will and taking up their cross. Today, I'm especially thankful for_____. In our Lord Jesus' Name. Amen.

THURSDAY

Read Luke 14:7–11.

1. What kind of a setting does Jesus picture here?

_____

_____

_____

_____

2. Where was He when He gave this instruction (see Luke 14:1–6)?

_____

_____

_____

_____

3. What elements in His instructions seem counter-cultural in our society?

_____

_____

_____

_____

4. Before John had spent several months with Jesus, where would he have most likely sat? How do you know?

_____

_____

_____

_____

5. What in this passage suggests that our humility may not go unnoticed?

_____

_____

_____

_____

6. What, according to Jesus' description here, should be our response if we take the lowest seat and no one seems to notice?

_____

_____

_____

_____

7. If the Lord is in a position to exalt those who voluntarily humble themselves, what do you think keeps most Christians from wearing the servant's mantle most of the time?

_____

_____

_____

_____

⌀ *Imitating the Master* ⌀

Jesus, I don't need to live my life in front of other people in hopes of being noticed or trying to impress them. My only responsibility in this life is to recognize that I have an audience of one and give You the performance of a lifetime. Remind me to trust You each day, Lord. In our Lord Jesus' Name. Amen.

FRIDAY

Read Revelation 1:9.

1. What two words does John use to describe himself to his readers?

    _____
    _____
    _____
    _____

2. In what way are these self-effacing terms?

    _____
    _____
    _____
    _____

3. Based on what the elderly apostle says about himself in this verse, which of the following do you think he is best able to teach you about? Why?
    • Tribulation
    • Kingdom
    • Patience
    • Jesus Christ

    _____
    _____
    _____
    _____

4. Other than a member of your immediate family, who else do you consider your "brothers and sisters"?

    _____
    _____
    _____
    _____

5. In what specific ways are those terms "brother" and "sister" more than just a handy means of address?

    _____
    _____
    _____
    _____

6. Why is that kind of relationship necessary in order to balance a life of love and truth?

    _____
    _____
    _____
    _____

7. With John's self-description in mind, how would those who know you best describe your view of yourself?

_____

_____

_____

_____

Imitating the Master

Lord Jesus, there is just something about "the apostle of love" that motivates me to be more like him. I appreciate his life of uncompromising devotion as well as the tenderness that resulted from walking with You and enduring hardship. Lord, make me willing to walk in John's sandals and draw on Your grace in order to reach the same destination he did. In our Lord Jesus' Name. Amen.

FOR LEADERS

(Notes and suggested answers for selected questions.)

ANOTHER LOOK

1. John's emphasis on love included:
   * The Christian's love for Christ
   * Christ's love for His church
   * The Christian's love for one another

2. In John's Gospel, he sets light against darkness, life against death, the kingdom of God against the kingdom of the devil, the children of God against the children of Satan, etc. In his epistles, he writes that we are either walking in the light or dwelling in the darkness. He also suggests that the person who is born of God does not sin, for we are either of God or of the world. For example, "Whoever transgresses and does not abide in the doctrine of Christ does not have God" (2 John 9).

3. On page 100, MacArthur writes that three years with Jesus transformed a self-centered fanatic into a mature man of balance and this Son of Thunder into the apostle of love."

4. The third epistle. The first half of this postcard-size communiqué is concerned with love. The second half references John's concern for orthodoxy and uncompromising loyalty to the truth of God.

5. "Take care of my mother." As far as we know, John was the only one of the Twelve who was actually at the crucifixion. But more than that, Jesus trusted him with the care of Mary because he had learned to be a humble, loving servant.

Imitating the Master

BIBLICAL CONNECTIONS

6. John is concerned with the overall pattern of person's life (and thus he emphasizes that righteousness should mark a believer's life). Paul, on the other hand, is concerned with exceptions that occur in a Christian's life because of the fact that we live in an imperfect world.

7. In the appearance of Moses and Elijah and the glorification of Jesus, the disciples witnessed the kingdom of God in a powerful way. Jesus wasn't speaking of an apocalyptic, end-of-the-world experience.

8. Not to talk about this great event was frustrating because John and James would have loved to add this to their list of achievements. It would have given them prestige among their peers. So that is the very reason they talked about it among themselves. At least in a small group they could try and milk this ego-boosting experience for everything it was worth.

9. In Mark 9:33 it is clear that Jesus did not ask the three what they were talking about among themselves because He didn't know. He already knew they were debating about which of them was greatest. He wanted to provide them with a means to confess their selfish actions. In Mark 9:38, it seems that John is convicted of his sectarianism when he hears Jesus extolling the virtues of servanthood. Here John voluntarily confesses to something of which he is guilty.

HIGHLIGHTING THE LESSON

11. He was lacking in love and compassion for people. He had to learn that knowing truth and living according to the truth of God's love were two different things.

13. In Mark 9, Jesus chided the Peter, James, and John about wanting to be important and then proceeded to teach the Twelve the need for them to become like children and live like servants. It is in this chapter where John confesses his weakness in this area. But in the very next chapter John and James are jockeying for preferential seating in heaven.

15. He alone witnessed the horror of Jesus' crucifixion. What is more, after serving the church in Ephesus he was exiled as an old man to the island of Patmos where he was forced to live in a cave in cruel conditions.

DAILY ASSIGNMENTS

Encourage the group participants not only to read the chapter in *Twelve Ordinary Men* assigned for the next lesson (chapter 6), but to use the Daily Assignments to review and remember the truth from God's Word you have just discussed.

Philip: The Dense Disciple Jesus Loved

BIBLICAL FOCUS

Key passages from this section of the book: Matthew 10:5–6; 15:24; John 1:11–12, 43–47; 6:1–7; 12:20–21; 14:1–11; 21:2–3; Romans 2:10; 1 Corinthians 1:27–29.

READING ASSIGNMENT

Read chapter 6 of *Twelve Ordinary Men.*

ANOTHER LOOK

The following questions will help you review the material you read in the book.

1. It is clear from various references that Peter, Andrew, James, and John were fisherman. But MacArthur writes, "There is good biblical evidence that Philip, Nathanael, and Thomas were all fisherman from Galilee" (p. 120). On what evidence does he base that conclusion?

   _____

   _____

   _____

   _____

2. Based on what MacArthur has pieced together about Philip from John's Gospel, which of the following labels is most apt to stick to this fisherman's lapel?
   • Possibility thinker
   • Process person
   • Change agent
   • Detail-challenged

3. In the author's words, "Peter, Andrew, and John (and likely James as well) had more or less found Jesus. To be precise, they had been directed to Him by John the Baptist" (p. 122). In light of this, what made Philip's encounter with Christ unique?

   _____

   _____

   _____

   _____

4. According to MacArthur, what might explain why the Greeks in John 12:20–21 sought out Philip (p. 128)?

_____

_____

_____

_____

5. For three years Philip had gazed into the very face of God and it still was not clear to him that to see Jesus was to see the Father. What does MacArthur suggest was the cause of Philip's lack of insight (p. 133)?

_____

_____

_____

_____

> Notice something interesting about the expression Philip uses with Nathanael: "We have found Him" As far as Philip was concerned, he had found the Messiah rather than being found by Him. Here we see the classic tension between sovereign election and human choice. Philip's call is a perfect illustration of how both exist in perfect harmony. The Lord found Philip, but Philip felt he found the Lord. Both things were true from the human perspective. But from a biblical perspective, we know that God's choice is the determinative one. "You did not choose Me, but I chose you and appointed you" (John 15:16).
>
> —*Twelve Ordinary Men*, p. 123

BIBLICAL CONNECTIONS

These questions will allow you to think through the biblical passages John MacArthur uses in this particular lesson.

6. In the above sidebar the author suggests that God takes the initiative when it comes to seeking out those with whom He desires a relationship. How is that principle illustrated in the following passages?
   • Jeremiah 1:4–5
   • Psalm 139:1–16
   • Ephesians 1:1–14

_____

_____

_____

_____

7. Nonetheless, when Philip encounters Nathanael, he is quick to claim that "we have found Him" (John 1:45). How do you make sense of this apparent contradiction?

_____

_____

_____

_____

8. Read John 6:1–7. It appears that the motive for Jesus' inquiry of Philip was a desire to test the disciple's faith. According to the following passages, what benefits are there to such episodes of testing?
   - 1 Peter 1:3–9
   - James 1:2–8
   - Psalm 139:23
   - 1 Timothy 3:10

_____

_____

_____

_____

9. It has been suggested that one of the reasons that Philip deferred to Andrew when some Greeks sought an audience with Jesus was his confusion about whether Gentiles were entitled to salvation. After all, Jesus had gone on record as saying, "Do not enter a city of the Samaritans. But go rather to the lost sheep of the house of Israel" (Matthew 10:5–6). He echoes the same thing in Matthew 15:24. In what way does Paul clarify this seeming exclusiveness (Romans 2:10)?

_____

_____

_____

_____

10. What do the following passages reveal about who God's redemption is intended for?
   - Genesis 12:1–3
   - John 1:11–12
   - Philippians 2:4–11
   - Revelation 7:9–10

_____

_____

_____

_____

WORD FOCUS

Philip is a Greek name, meaning "lover of horses." He must also have had a Jewish name, because all twelve apostles were Jewish. But his Jewish name is never given. Greek civilization had spread through the Mediterranean after the conquests of Alexander the Great in the fourth century B.C., and many people in the Middle East had adopted the Greek language, Greek culture, and Greek customs. They were known as "Hellenists" (cf. Acts 6:1). Perhaps Philip came from a family of Hellenistic Jews. Custom would have dictated that he have a Hebrew name as well, but for whatever reasons, he seems to have used his Greek name exclusively. So we know him only as Philip.

—*Twelve Ordinary Men, pp. 119–120*

HIGHLIGHTING THE LESSON

These questions have been designed to help you identify the central points MacArthur has made in this section of the book.

11. It's curious how Jesus went about choosing those who would represent Him on earth after He had returned to heaven. It wasn't a very representative group of individuals at all. Neither were they educated or theologically astute. Which of the following phrases would you say reflects what was important to Jesus? Why?
    - Beggars can't be choosers.
    - They were the best I could find.
    - At least they were willing.
    - Availability is more valuable that ability.

    _____

    _____

    _____

    _____

12. In spite of Philip's rough edges, he had a soft spot for truth. How is his seeking heart seen? In what way does Jesus celebrate this softness?

    _____

    _____

    _____

    _____

13. "Come and see," was Philip's counter to Nathanael's question about whether anything good can come out of Nazareth. Why was this response out of character for Philip? To what can you attribute this positive and adventuresome invitation?

_____

_____

_____

_____

_____

14. Philip's inability to escort the Greek seekers to Jesus on his own is consistent with his penchant for protocol and detail. And yet, what about this incident suggests that this "bean counter" wasn't entirely full of beans?

_____

_____

_____

_____

15. The fact that Philip wasn't cut from the starting lineup after failing his "Upper Room final" in systematic theology is good news for imperfect Christians. After three years of being personally trained by Jesus, Philip didn't understand that Jesus and the Father were one. Read John 14:7–11. What about Jesus' question to Philip suggests that faith is something a person must choose to act on?

_____

_____

_____

_____

One of the supreme essentials of leadership is a sense of vision—and this is especially true for anyone whose Master is Christ. But Philip was obsessed with mundane matters and therefore overwhelmed by the impossibility of the immediate problem. He knew too much arithmetic to be adventurous. The reality of the raw facts clouded his faith. He was so obsessed with this temporal predicament that he was oblivious to the transcendental possibilities that lay in Jesus' power. He was so enthralled with common-sense calculations that he didn't see the opportunity the situation presented. He should have said, "Lord, if You want to feed them, feed them. I'm just going to stand back and watch how you do it. I know You can do it, Lord. You made wine at Cana and fed Your children manna in the wilderness. Do it. We will tell everyone to get in line, and You just make the food." That would have been the right response. But Philip was convinced it simply couldn't be done. The limitless supernatural resources of Christ had completely escaped his thinking.

—*Twelve Ordinary Men*, p. 127

LASTING IMPLICATIONS

The following questions will assist you in drawing personal conclusions from God's Word.

16. At least half of the Twelve were from the same region and (in addition to the fact that they shared similar profession) were already friends. What about that scenario was a benefit to Jesus as He began to train these men?

_____

_____

_____

_____

17. Who was the first person Philip went to after Jesus tracked him down? Why might friendships be the best place to start in sharing your faith?

_____

_____

_____

_____

18. Philip was blind to the vision Jesus had for feeding the multitude. Can you think of a time in the life of your church where preoccupation with details prevented your leaders from seeing the big picture? Describe what happened.

_____

_____

_____

_____

19. Are you encouraged or appalled by the fact that Philip embarrassed himself in the Upper Room the night before Jesus died? Explain.

_____

_____

_____

_____

20. In what ways did Jesus challenge Philip's comfort zones? From what comfort zones does the Lord desire to remove you?

_____

_____

_____

_____

> Philip, like the other disciples, was a man of limited ability. He was a man of weak faith. He was a man of imperfect understanding. He was skeptical, analytical, pessimistic, reluctant, and unsure, He wanted to go by the book all the time. Facts and figures filled his thoughts. So he was unable to grasp the big picture of Christ's divine power, Person, and grace. He was slow to understand, slow to trust, and slow to see beyond the immediate circumstances. He still wanted more proof.
>
> —*Twelve Ordinary Men, p. 133*

DAILY ASSIGNMENTS

MONDAY

Read John 21:2–14.

1. In response to the mystery surrounding Jesus' death and resurrection, what does Peter feel like doing?

_____

_____

_____

_____

2. Based on the text, has Peter chosen an activity others are interested in pursuing? Why or why not?

_____

_____

_____

_____

3. The assumption is that Philip is among those who return to Galilee. If you had been in this situation, what activity would you probably have resorted to as a way of returning to "normal"?

_____

_____

_____

_____

4. What about this scene smacks of what was true of the Twelve before their encounter with Jesus?

_____

_____

_____

_____

5. True or false: Christians are a mixture of their pre-Christ and post-Christ selves. Explain your answer.

_____

_____

_____

_____

6. In what ways does your life continue to exhibit traces of habits and views you developed before you met Christ?

_____

_____

_____

_____

7. Based on how Jesus responded to His disciples on the lakeshore, what do you think He plans to do about your ongoing lifestyle?

_____

_____

_____

_____

❧ _Imitating the Master_ ❧

_Lord, forgive my tendency to fall back into old patterns You've delivered me from. Today I am especially aware of my weakness when it comes to _____. I accept Your forgiveness, but also ask for Your strength to resist when temptation strikes this week. In our Lord Jesus' Name I pray. Amen._

TUESDAY

Read John 1:43 and 21:19–22.

1. Compare the two situations described in these passages. What is similar? What is different?

_____

_____

_____

_____

2. Who were the participants in each event?

_____

_____

_____

_____

3. In Philip's case, Jesus was literally asking Philip to follow Him as He returned to Galilee. What did the phrase "Follow Me" imply for Philip in John 1?

_____
_____
_____
_____

4. What did the phrase, "Follow Me" imply for Peter (John 21)?

_____
_____
_____
_____

5. How is this phrase a way of explaining what it means to be a Christian?

_____
_____
_____
_____

6. Jesus knew that Philip was a fallible individual before He called him. (Peter had demonstrated that he was fallible prior to the John 21 scene.) Still Jesus wanted them to follow. Is that encouraging or convicting as you review your obedience this past week? Explain.

_____
_____
_____
_____

7. When was the last time you sensed Jesus speaking to you about a decision or choice in your life and saying, "Follow Me"?

_____
_____
_____
_____

✑ *Imitating the Master* ✑

Jesus, don't ever let me get over the wonder that You called me to follow You. It is easy to lose sight of what that invitation implies. You love me. You have a plan for me. You desire to spend time with me. Oh, Jesus, I'm not deserving of being invited to be with You, but I don't want to be anywhere else. In our Lord Jesus' Name. Amen.

WEDNESDAY

Read John 6:5–10.

1. Why did Jesus ask Philip where they could find food for the gathered crowd?

_____

_____

_____

_____

2. What did Philip reply?

_____

_____

_____

_____

3. How would you characterize the manner in which Philip responded?

_____

_____

_____

_____

4. Would you say Philip passed this "test of faith"? Why or why not?

_____

_____

_____

_____

5. What is an impossible situation you are currently facing that you are reluctant to trust the Lord for?

_____

_____

_____

_____

6. What do you think is the basis of your reluctance?

_____

_____

_____

_____

7. What could Jesus be planning by allowing that challenge to come into your life?

_____

_____

_____

You know, Lord, I'm glad You weren't too hard on Philip. You wired him to be a nuts-and-bolts kind of guy because You needed his organizational skills. But You still gave him a lesson he never forgot. Help me never to forget the situations You allow me to experience where I see Your amazing provision up close and personal. In our Lord Jesus' Name. Amen.

THURSDAY

Read John 14:1–11.

1. What does Jesus reveal about Himself in this passage?

_____

_____

_____

_____

2. What does He reveal about His intentions?

_____

_____

_____

_____

3. How confident does Jesus seem that His disciples understand what He is talking about?

_____

_____

_____

_____

4. Does Philip's lack of understanding surprise you? Why or why not?

_____

_____

_____

_____

5. If knowledge of the Father is equated with knowledge of Jesus, what spiritual disciplines can Christians engage in if they desire to truly know God?

_____

_____

_____

_____

6. What does "spending time with the Lord" mean in your life right now?

_____

_____

_____

7. If spending time with the Lord is not sufficient (obviously it wasn't for Philip), what safeguards will make your own time with the Lord have its desired effect?

_____

_____

_____

_____

❧ Imitating the Master ❧

Jesus, I'd like to think that if I'd been in the Upper Room that night I could have clued Philip in as to who You were and what You were talking about. But before I brag too much I remember how Peter claimed that he would die for You. So instead Lord, I'm just going to call out to You and confess just how failure-prone and slow to understand I am. Accept me Lord and help me grow in You.

In our Lord Jesus' Name. Amen.

FRIDAY

Read 1 Corinthians 1:27–29.

1. Based on what this text says, how does God consider "weak" and "foolish" people?

_____

_____

_____

_____

2. How does God's choice of servants compare with the way we determine the worthiness of other people?

_____

_____

_____

_____

3. Of all the reasons Paul gives to explain God's strategy, what is the ultimate reason that God delights in utilizing those He chooses?

_____

_____

_____

_____

4. Based on what you know of Philip, is he a good illustration of the truth of this passage? Why or why not?

_____

_____

5. When do you feel least qualified to be recognized as a follower of Christ?

_____

_____

_____

_____

6. When you feel most qualified, what is going on in your life that prompts that confidence?

_____

_____

_____

_____

7. What's the difference between reasonable and humble confidence on the one hand, and dangerous pride on the other?

_____

_____

_____

_____

✑ Imitating the Master ✑

Lord Jesus, I often wish I could have had the faith-boosting experience of literally sitting at Your feet. But even those who had that enviable privilege often misunderstood You. Sometimes I don't understand everything either. Help me continue to trust Your ways in my life, Lord. In our Lord Jesus' Name. Amen.

FOR LEADERS

(Notes and suggested answers for selected questions.)

ANOTHER LOOK

1. In John 21, after the resurrection when the apostles returned to Galilee and Peter said, "I am going fishing" (John 21:3), the others who were there all answered "We are going with you also." According to John 21:2, that group included Thomas and Nathanael. And based on implication, the other two unnamed disciples were Philip and Andrew. When the others are named elsewhere as being together, these two are also included.

2. Definitely a "process person." From what we find in John's Gospel, Philip is a "bean counter." He's a by-the-book, practical minded, non-forward-

thinking type of individual. He is someone who is obsessed with identifying reasons things can't be done rather than finding ways to do them.

3. Philip was the first person to whom Jesus ever said, "Follow Me."

4. He had a Greek name.

5. His full appreciation of whose presence he had enjoyed was severely limited by his earthbound thinking, his materialism, his skepticism, his obsession with mundane details, his preoccupation with business details, and his small-mindedness.

BIBLICAL CONNECTIONS

6. The Jeremiah passage celebrates God's foreknowledge and the fact that He earmarked the prophet for a special ministry before he was born. In Psalms and Ephesians we see a similar emphasis. God is the "first mover."

7. From a divine point of view, God always finds us. But from a human point of view, we interpret such encounters from our own vantage point.

8. Testing reveals:
   • 1 Peter 1:3–9—The genuineness of faith
   • James 1:2–8—The development of perseverance
   • Psalms 139:23—The anxiousness of our hearts
   • 1 Timothy 3:10—Readiness for service

9. Although Jesus' primary thrust in His ministry was to reach the Jews, this should be understood only as an issue of priority. The Greeks (or non-Jews) were always part of God's redemptive agenda.

10. In each of these passages, God's heartbeat for the world is unmistakable.

HIGHLIGHTING THE LESSON

11. Availability is more valuable than ability. Jesus can train those who are willing and open.

12. Philip was in the wilderness following after John the Baptist when Jesus found him. In addition to that, Philip obviously was a student of the Scriptures because he makes reference to the books of Moses when he tells Nathanael that he thinks Jesus is the Messiah. Jesus obviously was impressed. He invited him to follow Him and in the end, He chose him as one of the Twelve.

13. You would think Philip's cautious manner would prevent him from taking the lead in a situation like this. It is more likely that he would have picked up on Nathanael's reticence and dropped the topic right away. But he didn't. There is no other explanation for this change of heart than "a change of heart" that Jesus was bringing about by His grace.

14. He didn't let the issue drop. He found Andrew in order that the strangers would get their desire. Philip had a heart for what was right (even if he couldn't quite explain why this was a right thing to do).

DAILY ASSIGNMENTS

Encourage the group participants not only to read the chapter in *Twelve Ordinary Men* assigned for the next lesson (chapter 7), but to use the Daily Assignments to review and remember the truth from God's Word you have just discussed.

8

Nathanael: Purely Prejudice

BIBLICAL FOCUS

Key passages from this section of the book: Matthew 23:13–33; Luke 4:22–29; John 1:43–51; 7:52; 2 Romans 2:28–9; 9:6–7; Corinthians 4:3–4.

READING ASSIGNMENT

Read chapter 7 of *Twelve Ordinary Men.*

ANOTHER LOOK

The following questions will help you review the material you read in the book.

1. According to MacArthur, Nathanael and Philip were good friends. Other than the fact that their names are linked in each of the synoptic lists of the Twelve, on what does he base this statement?

   _____
   _____
   _____
   _____

2. MacArthur states, "They [Jesus' disciples] were very different from the religious establishment" (p. 137). What did he mean by this?

   _____
   _____
   _____
   _____

3. Jesus is an Aramaic name. What is its equivalent in Hebrew? And what does that Hebrew name mean (p. 138)?

   _____
   _____
   _____
   _____

4. "It is inconceivable to Nathanael that the Messiah would come out of a tacky place like Nazareth" (p. 140). On what does the author base this statement?

_____

_____

_____

_____

5. According to MacArthur, it was prejudice that skewed the view of Jesus' contemporaries from being able to see Him as the Messiah. What were the three kinds of prejudice the author identifies?

_____

_____

_____

_____

Incidentally, it appears that all the apostles, with the exception of Judas Iscariot, were to some degree already true seekers after divine truth before they met Jesus. They were already being drawn by the Spirit of God. Their hearts were open to the truth and hungry to know it. They were sincere in their love for God and their desire to know the truth and receive the Messiah. In that sense they were very different from the religious establishment, which was dominated by hypocrisy and false piety. The disciples were the real thing.

—*Twelve Ordinary Men, p. 137*

BIBLICAL CONNECTIONS

These questions will allow you to think through the biblical passages John MacArthur uses in this particular lesson

6. When John the Baptist pointed to Jesus and declared Him to be the Lamb of God who takes away the sin of the world, those who heard him understood what he was referring to. Based on the following passages in the Old Testament, what symbol does the "lamb" suggest?

   • Genesis 22:1–14

   _____

   _____

   • Exodus 12:21–23

   _____

   _____

   • Leviticus 4:32–35

   _____

- Leviticus 16:10

7. In John 1:46, Nathanael's response betrays a latent bias against people from Nazareth. This is but one recorded evidence of Jesus being the object of prejudice. There are several in Scripture. What "prejudicial" assumptions are made against Jesus in the following verses? In what way are they similar to the ways people are discriminated against today?

- John 7:52

- Luke 4:22

- Isaiah 53:1-3

 WORD FOCUS

Jesus refers to him as "an Israelite indeed." The word in the Greek text is *alethos*, meaning "truly, genuinely." He was an authentic Israelite.

This is not a reference to his physical descent from Abraham. Jesus was not talking about genetics. He was linking Nathanael's status as a true Israelite to the fact that he was without deceit. His guilelessness is what defined him as a true Israelite. For the most part, the Israelites of Jesus' day were not real, because they were hypocrites. They were phonies. They lived life with a veneer of spirituality, but it was not real, and therefore they were not genuine spiritual sons of Abraham. Nathanael, however, was real.

In Romans 9:6–7, the apostle Paul says, "For they are not all Israel who are of Israel, nor are they all children because they are the seed of Abraham." In Romans 2:28–29, he writes, "He is not a Jew who is one outwardly, nor is circumcision that which is outward in the flesh; but he is a Jew who is one inwardly; and circumcision is that of the heart, in the Spirit, not in the letter; whose praise is not from men but from God."

Here was an authentic Jew, one of the true spiritual offspring of Abraham. Here was one who worshiped the true and living God without deceit and without hypocrisy. Nathanael was the authentic item. Jesus would later say in John 8:31, "If you abide in My word, you are My disciples indeed." The Greek word is the same—*alethos*.

—*Twelve Ordinary Men, p. 143*

8. Read Matthew 23:13–33. In contrast to the sincerity of faith that is portrayed in Nathanael (as described in the above sidebar), the religious leaders of Jesus' day were *"alethos* challenged." What of the following phrases captures the essence of their hypocrisy? (Circle one).

- "Do as I say, not as I do."
- "God looks on the outward appearance; man looks on the heart."
- "Nobody's perfect."
- "Gimme a break! I'm doing the best I can!"

9. Read Luke 2:25–32. Although Simeon was much older than Nathanael, and although the former met Jesus much earlier than Nathanael did, what was true of both of these men and their responses to Jesus?

_____

_____

_____

_____

10. When Jesus encountered Nathanael, He said to him, "Most assuredly, I say to you, hereafter you shall see heaven open, and the angels of God ascending and descending upon the Son of Man" (John 1:51). The meaning of this metaphor can only be understood by looking at the Old Testament passage Jesus had in mind. After reading Genesis 28:12, do your best to explain what Jesus is saying about Himself.

_____

_____

_____

_____

HIGHLIGHTING THE LESSON

These questions have been designed to help you identify the central points MacArthur has made in this section of the book.

11. Nathanael was interested in the fulfillment of prophecy. Based on how Philip referenced Jesus to him, it was obvious he had devoted time to study and reflection of Moses' writings and those of the prophets. Does this surprise you considering that Nathanael most likely was a fisherman? Why or why not?

_____

_____

_____

_____

12. Jesus called attention to Nathanael's personal discipline of studying and reflecting on the Scripture. According to MacArthur, that's what Jesus was referring to when He said, "Before Philip called you, when you were under the fig tree, I saw you" (John 1:48). Why did the author suggest that this figure of speech meant that Nathanael was given to personal prayer and reflection (p. 145)?

_____

_____

_____

_____

_____

13. In spite of Nathanael's devotion to Scripture, he was not devoid of personal imperfection. What was his signature sin? Why would the fact that Nathanael was raised in Cana contribute to the irrational nature of prejudice?

_____

_____

_____

_____

14. Given the fact that Nathanael sometimes falsely categorized people, how is it that Jesus recognized him as one who did not have deceit in his heart (John 1:47)? Which of the following offers the best explanation for this apparent contradiction?

- "In spite of what I say, I really want to please you, Lord."
- "If you think I'm prejudiced now, Jesus, you should have seen me when . . ."
- "Lord, I know I'm sinful. My tender heart convicts me all the time."
- "You think I'm without deceit? Boy, have I fooled you, Jesus."

15. From the start, Nathanael confessed, "Rabbi, You are the Son of God! You are the King of Israel!" (John 1:49). What was it that led him to this conclusion from day one, when Philip still didn't recognize it after three years of walking with Jesus?

_____

_____

_____

_____

John Bunyan understood the danger of prejudice. In his famous allegory, *The Holy War,* he pictures the forces of Immanuel coming to bring the gospel to the town of Mansoul. They directed their assault on Mansoul at the Ear-gate, because faith comes by hearing. But Diabolus, the enemy of Immanuel and His forces, wanted to hold Mansoul captive to hell. So Diabolus decided to meet the attack by stationing a special guard at Ear-gate. The guard he chose was "one old Mr. Prejudice, an angry and ill-conditioned fellow." According to Bunyan, they made Mr. Prejudice "captain of the ward at that gate, and put under his power sixty men, called deaf men; men advantageous for that service, forasmuch as they mattered no words of the captains, nor of the soldiers." That is a very vivid description of precisely how many people are rendered impervious to the truth of the gospel. Their own prejudice renders them deaf to the truth.

—Twelve Ordinary Men, p. 141

LASTING IMPLICATIONS

The following questions will assist you in drawing personal conclusions from God's Word.

16. When Philip told Nathanael that he had found Jesus, he didn't say, "I've found a man who has a wonderful plan for your life" or "someone who can fix your marriage." How did he present Jesus as One for whom they'd been looking?

_____

_____

_____

_____

17. Why is it the norm today to offer Jesus as someone who can meet felt needs instead of someone who is the essence of the Truth?

_____

_____

_____

_____

18. What prejudices do the people in your sphere of influence tend to have? Are these as irrational as the one Nathanael struggled with? Why or why not?

_____

_____

_____

_____

19. What can Nathanael teach us about where the ideal place might be to spend time with the Lord?

_____

_____

_____

_____

DAILY ASSIGNMENTS

MONDAY

Read John 1:43–47.

1. What in the passage suggests that Philip had a preexisting relationship with Nathanael?

_____

_____

_____

_____

What was the significance of the fig tree? It was most likely the place where Nathanael went to study and meditate on Scripture. Houses in that culture were mostly small, one-room affairs. Most of the cooking was done inside, so a fire was kept burning even in the summer. The house could get full of smoke and stuffy. Trees were planted around houses to keep them cool and shaded. One of the best trees to plant near a house was a fig tree, because it bore wonderful fruit and gave good shade. Fig trees grow to a height of only about fifteen feet. They have a fairly short, gnarled trunk, and their branches are low and spread as far as twenty-five- or thirty feet. A fig tree near a house provided a large, shady, protected place outdoors. If you wanted to escape the noise and stifling atmosphere of the house, you could go outside and rest under its shade. It was a kind of private outdoor place, perfect for meditation, reflection, and solitude. No doubt that is where Nathanael went to study Scripture and pray.

—Twelve Ordinary Men, p. 145

2. In what ways do these verses suggest that Nathanael was ready to respond to Jesus?

_____

_____

_____

_____

3. For both Philip and Nathanael it took "personal study" and "being asked" to trigger their commitment. Based on your observations, are these two qualities always crucial in someone's surrendering to Christ? Why or why not?

_____

_____

_____

_____

4. What would you say were the two or three most significant hurdles God took you over on your way to commitment to Christ?

_____

_____

_____

_____

5. What individual has been like Philip for you? In other words, who came alongside you and suggested you check out Jesus for yourself?

_____

_____

_____

_____

6. What caused you to trust that invitation?

_____

_____

_____

_____

7. For whom have you been a Philip? In whose life might God use you in that role on their way to faith?

_____

_____

_____

_____

❧ *Imitating the Master* ❧

Lord, as I read about Philip and Nathanael, I think about my relationship with _____. Thank You for that person's influence in my life. My prayer is that we would continue to be mutually involved in each other's spiritual growth. Please encourage him/her today. In our Lord Jesus' Name. Amen.

TUESDAY

Read John 1:43–47.

1. What did Philip say to appease Nathanael's curiosity and doubt?

_____

_____

_____

_____

2. How did Nathanael respond to Philip's invitation?

_____

_____

_____

_____

3. Does his response surprise you? Why or why not?

_____

_____

_____

_____

4. What principle can be extracted from this passage about dealing with people who know what you believe but aren't sure about it themselves?

_____

_____

_____

5. Under what circumstances would it be appropriate to say to a neighbor or friend, "Come and see what you think about the place I go to church"?

_____

_____

_____

_____

6. What did Nathanael's readiness to take the next step reveal about his character?

_____

_____

_____

_____

7. In light of that, how could you advance a neighbor's readiness little by little?

_____

_____

_____

_____

✑ Imitating the Master ✑

Jesus, forgive me that I clam up when the time is right to pique the curiosity of those I've earned the right to share with. Give me the courage and a sense of timing to invite _____ to church with me. But besides Sunday worship, there are other ways that I can move those You've brought into my life closer to You. Show me tangible ways I can say, "Come and see what means so much to me."
In our Lord Jesus' Name. Amen.

WEDNESDAY

Read John 1:47–51.

1. What does verse 47 imply about Nathanael's ultimate response to Philip's invitation in verse 46?

_____

_____

_____

_____

2. What did Jesus observe before He actually spoke to Nathanael?

_____

_____

_____

_____

3. Does it seem that Nathanael was surprised by Jesus' affirming words to him? Why or why not?

_____

_____

_____

_____

4. How would you have reacted if Jesus had said those words to you?

_____

_____

_____

_____

5. Being known as a person who is "truly" God's own and in whose heart there is no deceit doesn't require you to be sinless. What does it require?

_____

_____

_____

_____

6. Would you say you are a person who is without deceit? What would people who know you say? Explain.

_____

_____

_____

_____

7. Are you more like Philip or Nathanael? Explain.

_____

_____

_____

_____

∂ *Imitating the Master* ∂

You know, Lord, it's difficult to read this passage of Scripture without seeing how You go out of Your way to reward those who take baby steps of faith toward You. I want to be more quick to "go for it" when I sense what You are calling me to do. But I need Your help, Lord, just like Nathanael needed Philip's encouraging prompting. In our Lord Jesus' Name. Amen.

Read 2 Corinthians 4:3–4.

1. Whereas John Bunyan used the metaphor of deafness (in the sidebar), how does Paul describe those who resist God's truth in this passage?

_____

_____

_____

_____

2. How does each comparison illustrate an aspect of resistance to God?

_____

_____

_____

_____

3. Who does Bunyan credit with being the culprit?

_____

_____

_____

_____

4. What does the "god of this age" do to blind us through issues of prejudice (as represented by his influence in our culture)?

_____

_____

_____

_____

5. How would you describe the remedy for this blindness (or deafness)?

_____

_____

_____

_____

6. When have you felt you were the victim of prejudicial thinking?

_____

_____

_____

_____

7. What about Nathanael's experience indicates that it is very easy to be prejudiced toward others who are, in reality, not all that different from you?

_____

_____

_____

_____

Jesus, if I am battling any kind of prejudice in my heart, reveal it to me.
Then cleanse me from that sin so that I will be living in obedience to You.
In our Lord Jesus' Name. Amen.

FRIDAY

Read John 2:25.

1. What does this verse suggest Jesus can do?

    _____

    _____

    _____

    _____

2. How did He demonstrate His ability in His encounter with Nathanael?

    _____

    _____

    _____

    _____

3. What are the possible reactions a person might have to Jesus' complete knowledge of him or her (from a distance)?

    _____

    _____

    _____

    _____

4. If Jesus were to have said to you that He saw you under the fig tree reading, would you be pleased that He knew the kind of material you tend to read? Why or why not?

    _____

    _____

    _____

    _____

5. How does the fact that nothing in you is hidden from God's sight affect your sense of personal privacy?

    _____

    _____

    _____

    _____

6. How should Jesus' omniscience affect the way Christians pray?

_____

_____

_____

_____

7. Describe one quality of Nathanael you would like God to build into your life.

_____

_____

_____

_____

❧ *Imitating the Master* ❧

Lord Jesus, You know all about me from the inside out. That is at once terribly frightening and wonderfully comforting. Lord, I am in need of Your help to revise the way I spend my discretionary time. You know I spend entirely too much time _____. Beginning today, help me revise my use of time so I can maximize moments with You. In our Lord Jesus' Name. Amen.

FOR LEADERS

(Notes and suggested answers for selected questions.)

ANOTHER LOOK

1. According to John 1:45, after Jesus called Philip to follow Him, we are told that Philip immediately went to tell Nathanael. Why else would he do this unless they were close?

2. The religious establishment was dominated by hypocrisy and false piety while the disciples (with the exception of Judas) had hearts that were open to the truth and hungry to know it. According to the author, "They were sincere in their love for God and their desire to know the truth" (p. 137).

3. In Hebrew, Jesus' name is Joshua, which means "Yahweh is salvation."

4. The author states that Nazareth was an uncultured place, full of evil, corrupt, and populated with sinful people.

5. The prejudice was directed at Jesus because:
   A. He was a Galilean and a Nazarene.
   B. He was an uneducated person outside the religious establishment.
   C. His message offended them.

BIBLICAL CONNECTIONS

6. In each case the lamb is the required sacrifice for the forgiveness of sin.

7. Here are what we learn:
    A. John 7:52 exposes a bias against people from Galilee (lower class).
    B. Luke 4:22 exposes a bias against carpenters (commoners).
    C. Isaiah 53:1-3 exposes a bias against the unpopular and unattractive.

8. The best answer is "A."

9. They both were students of the Scriptures and were looking for the Messiah. They both readily responded when they met Jesus for the first time.

10. Jesus is the "ladder." He alone is the means by which we reach the Father.

HIGHLIGHTING THE LESSON

12. In these days, most of the cooking was done indoors so trees were planted outside to provide a cool shaded place to which to retreat. A fig tree grew to fifteen feet and was a wonderful location for reflection away from the heat and hurry of the activities in the home.

13. His comment about Nazareth indicates he was down on "Nazarenes." Cana was just as much on the wrong side of the tracks as Nazareth. It doesn't make sense that Nathanael would put down a group of people who were no different from him.

15. He recognized the supernatural power of Jesus' omniscience.

DAILY ASSIGNMENTS

Encourage the group participants not only to read the chapter in *Twelve Ordinary Men* assigned for the next lesson (chapter 8), but to use the Daily Assignments to review and remember the truth from God's Word you have just discussed.

9

4. MacArthur says this about Thomas: "He is usually nicknamed 'Doubting Thomas,' but that may not be the most fitting label for him. He was a better man than the popular lore would indicate" (p. 157). Still, Thomas did have a personality quirk that causes the author to liken him to what character in "Winnie the Pooh"?

_____

_____

_____

_____

5. Following Thomas's encounter with Jesus after the resurrection, MacArthur describes the scene. "Then Thomas made what was probably the greatest statement ever to come from the lips of the apostles: 'My Lord and my God!' . . . Let those who question the deity of Christ meet Thomas. Suddenly, Thomas's melancholy, comfortless, negative, moody tendencies were forever banished. . ." (p. 164). What does the author contend was the cause of this dramatic personality change?

_____

_____

_____

_____

> But what irritated the religious leaders was not the miracles. They could have lived with the fact that He could walk on water or that He could make food to feed thousands of people. What they could not tolerate was being called sinners. They would *not* acknowledge themselves as poor, prisoners, bline, and oppressed (Luke 4:18). They were too smugly self-righteous. So when Jesus came (as John the Baptist had come before Him) preaching repentance and saying they were sinners, wretched, poor, blind, lost people under the bondage of their own iniquity, needing forgiveness and cleansing—they could not and would not tolerate that. Therefore it was ultimately because of His *message* that they hated Him, vlified Him, and finally executed Him.
>
> That is precisely why when it came time for Him to appoint apostles, He chose lowly, ordinary men. They were men who were not reluctant to acknowledge their own sinfulness.
>
> —*Twelve Ordinary Men, pp. 150–151*

These questions will allow you to think through the biblical passages John MacArthur uses in this particular lesson.

6. In the above sidebar, the author links the verses of Isaiah that Jesus read in the synagogue with those who were in attendance. Ironically, this description of the Messiah's mission was intended to be good news. Based on MacArthur's interpretation, why was it received as bad news? Read Luke 4:18–19 as well as Isaiah 61:1–2.

_____

_____

_____

_____

7. Jesus deliberately passed over those who were aristocratic and influential and chose men mostly from the dregs of society. But according to the author, "That is how it has always been in God's economy" (p. 149). What comes through loud and clear in the following passages of Scripture? Psalm 8:2

_____

_____

Isaiah 26:5-6

_____

_____

Ezekiel 21:26

_____

_____

Zephaniah 3:12

_____

_____

8. Apparently Jesus had a special place in His heart for tax collectors. How do the following references confirm or contradict that impression?
• Matthew 9:9–13; 21:31–32

_____

_____

• Luke 7:29; 15:1; 18:10–14; 19:2–10

_____

_____

9. Read John 11:4–16. In verses 5 and 6, the author points out an interesting juxtaposition of thoughts. What is it? What principle about God's way versus man's way can you glean from the way the story actually concludes? State that principle in a headline for the *Jerusalem Post-Gazette*.

_____
_____
_____
_____

10. Although Thomas is often called "the doubter" (based on his comments in John 20:25), what in the following verses suggests that others might be just as deserving of that label? What in the verses gives you reason to identify with these "ordinary men"?

Mark 16:10–11

_____
_____

Mark 16:13

_____
_____

John 20:20

_____
_____

 WORD FOCUS

There were two kinds of tax collectors, the *Gabbai* and the *Mokhes*. The Gabbai were general tax collectors. They collected property tax, income tax, and the poll tax. These taxes were set by official assessments, so there was not as much graft at this level. The Mokhes, however, collected a duty on imports and exports, goods for domestic trade, and virtually anything that was moved by road. They set tolls on roads and bridges, they taxed beasts of burden and axles on transport wagons, and they charged a tariff on parcels, letters, and whatever else they could find to tax. Their assessments were often arbitrary and capricious.

—*Twelve Ordinary Men, p. 154*

These questions have been designed to help you identify the central points MacArthur has made in this section of the book.

11. What was Matthew's first impulse after Jesus invited him to follow?

_____

_____

_____

_____

12. Whom did Matthew invite to be part of his celebration? What are you inclined to view as a transferable principle in this "paradigm of conversion"?

_____

_____

_____

_____

> We know that Matthew knew the Old Testament very well, because his Gospel quotes the Old Testament ninety-nine times. That is more times than Mark, Luke, and John combined. Matthew obviously had extensive familiarity with the Old Testament. In fact, he quotes out of the Law, out of the Psalms, and out of the Prophets—every section of the Old Testament. So he had a good working knowledge of all the Scriptures that were available to him. He must have pursued his study of the Old Testament on his own, because he couldn't hear the Word of God explained in any synagogue. Apparently, in a quest to fill the spiritual void in his life, he had turned to the Scriptures.
>
> —*Twelve Ordinary Men, pp. 155–156*

13. The immediacy of Matthew's response is remarkable when you consider that he left his toll booth standing in the middle of the road. What can you assume about this notorious tax collector as you make sense of his irreversible decision?

_____

_____

_____

_____

14. MacArthur describes Thomas as pessimistic. But he doesn't leave it at that. He suggests that our first peek into the personality of this man (John 11:16) should alert us to his pessimistic heroism. What does he mean by this? What does it suggest about Thomas?

_____

_____

_____
_____

15. Thomas was not present with the other disciples when Jesus first entered the Upper Room after the resurrection (pp. 162–163). What about his personality would explain his desire to be alone?

_____
_____
_____
_____

LASTING IMPLICATIONS

The following questions will assist you in drawing personal conclusions from God's Word.

16. Apparently what separated the men Jesus overlooked from the boys He called to be His followers was their willingness to admit to their own sinfulness. If forgiveness and unconditional love are the payout for such a confession, why did so many people try to cover up their need for Christ then? What about now?

_____
_____
_____
_____

17. Matthew threw a huge party for Jesus at his home. He invited his notorious friends in order to introduce them to his newest friend. In what ways might a home be a perfect place of hospitality and ministry?

_____
_____
_____
_____

18. For this tax collector, hosting a dinner party for Jesus was his way of acknowledging that a change had occurred in his heart. What other tangible ways can you think of that would signal "salvation has come to this house" (as recorded about Zacchaeus in Luke 19:9)?

_____
_____
_____
_____

19. As cautious as this pessimist was, Thomas was the first one to suggest that all the disciples go with Jesus to Bethany, even though it meant walking into enemy territory. What did this seem to suggest about faith in Christ?

_____
_____
_____
_____

20. There is no indication that the disciples in the Upper Room were bent out of shape over the fact that Thomas was not with them. How important is it to allow people space to deal with their feelings when they think that people (or God) have disappointed them? What tact would you take with someone like Thomas?

_____
_____
_____
_____

> Thomas was devoted to Christ. He may have been the equal to John in this regard. When we think about someone who loved Jesus and was intimate with Him, we usually think of John, because he was always near Jesus. But it is clear from this account that Thomas did not want to live without Jesus. If Jesus was going to die, Thomas was prepared to die with Him. In essence he says, "Guys, suck it up; let's go and die. Better to die and be with Christ than to be left behind."
>
> —*Twelve Ordinary Men, p. 161*

DAILY ASSIGNMENTS

MONDAY

Read Luke 5:29–32.

1. Who were the invited and the party-crashers at the feast Matthew (Levi) hosted?

_____
_____
_____
_____

2. What was the complaint of the scribes and Pharisees?

_____
_____
_____
_____

3. How would you express a contemporary version of this same complaint?

_____

_____

_____

_____

4. How did Jesus defend His willingness to spend time in such a setting?

_____

_____

_____

_____

5. Based on the metaphor Jesus employed, can you draw the implication from this that every person is spiritually sick? Why or why not?

_____

_____

_____

_____

6. How does Jesus' concern for those who need a "physician" challenge you in your choices of who to socialize with?

_____

_____

_____

_____

7. Describe the most unusual place you have ever found yourself as a result of attempting to influence your world for Christ.

_____

_____

_____

_____

✧ Imitating the Master ✧

Lord, I'm convicted by Matthew's willingness to introduce his non-Christian friends to You. I'm bothered by the fact that I don't have that many friends who don't go to church. Open my heart to the needs of those around me. Give me Your desire to spend time with "spiritually sick" people. I want my home to be a place of ministry to those You will bring into my life. In our Lord Jesus' Name I pray. Amen.

Read Luke 18:9–14.

1. Where did the tax collector stand as he prayed?

_____

_____

_____

_____

2. Based on what you've learned about tax collectors, why was this so?

_____

_____

_____

_____

3. How and where did the Pharisee stand? Why?

_____

_____

_____

_____

4. Being grateful that the Lord has given you blessings and opportunities others have not had isn't wrong. But what was it about the Pharisee's prayer that wasn't right?

_____

_____

_____

_____

5. What was it about the tax collector's prayer that made it so acceptable in God's sight?

_____

_____

_____

_____

6. Complete this sentence: I am more likely to be like the Pharisee in this parable when I _____.

_____

_____

_____

_____

7. Complete this sentence: I am more likely to be like the tax collector in this parable when I _____.

_____

_____

_____

Jesus, there is something refreshing about the prayer of the sin-conscious tax collector. There is no pretense. He has nothing to prove. But he desperately desires to draw near to You. That's my desire, Lord. Help me keep short accounts with You starting today. In our Lord Jesus' Name. Amen.

WEDNESDAY

Read Matthew 22:21 and Romans 13:7.

1. What is the purpose of taxation?

_____

_____

_____

_____

2 What is a Christian's responsibility to the government when it comes to paying taxes?

_____

_____

_____

_____

3. Why would a tax collector be held at arm's length by the Jews?

_____

_____

_____

_____

4. What would be your first thought if you opened a letter from the government and read the following: "Congratulations, you've just been chosen for an IRS audit"?

_____

_____

_____

_____

5. What do you think it would be like to have a job that exposes you to the instant suspicion and hatred of others?

_____

_____

_____

_____

6. How might a person's frustration with his or her job actually result in an openness to the gospel?

_____
_____
_____
_____

7. What about your work sets you up to be misjudged by peers? How does that tension affect your day-to-day experience of God's presence in your life?

_____
_____
_____
_____

✑ *Imitating the Master* ✑

You know what I like about my job, Jesus. You also know what I have trouble with. This week I am frustrated by _____. Still, I am grateful to be employed. As long as You have me at this place of employment, I want to represent You by my attitudes and actions. In our Lord Jesus' Name. Amen.

THURSDAY

Read John 11:1–16.

1. List the participants in these dramatic moments with a one-sentence description of each one's part in the events.

_____
_____
_____
_____

2. What surprises you about Jesus in this passage?

_____
_____
_____
_____

3. Based on what you thought you knew about Thomas, what surprises you about him in these verses?

_____
_____
_____
_____

4. What proof is there that Thomas was the obvious leader in this situation?

_____

_____

_____

_____

5. How would you describe someone you know who, if he or she suggested you join in doing something daring, you'd follow in a heartbeat?

_____

_____

_____

_____

6. What is it about some people that makes them "followable" in that way?

_____

_____

_____

_____

7. In what circumstances do you think you would be willing to die for your faith?

_____

_____

_____

_____

❧ *Imitating the Master* ❧

Jesus, just as I was impressed by the humility of the repentant tax collector, I'm inspired by Thomas's courage to die with You. I'm also impressed with the fact that he could convince the other disciples to follow his advice. Lord, I want to be a person of courage and influence among those with whom I live, work, and worship.
In our Lord Jesus' Name. Amen.

FRIDAY

Read John 20:19–29.

1. What did Jesus do that caused the disciples to recognize Him almost immediately?

_____

_____

_____

_____

2. Exactly what conditions did Thomas require of Jesus before he could believe the Resurrection?

_____

_____

_____

_____

3. How do you explain Jesus' gentleness with Thomas?

_____

_____

_____

_____

4. What does Jesus say to Thomas that challenges him not to rely so much on physical proofs?

_____

_____

_____

_____

5. How does Thomas respond when he realizes the person standing before him really is the risen Christ?

_____

_____

_____

6. Do you think Thomas was spooked or encouraged by the fact that Jesus knew about his secret doubts?

_____

_____

_____

7. How should the fact that the risen Christ is everywhere present even though we don't see Him elevate an ordinary disciple to an extraordinary one?

_____

_____

_____

❧ *Imitating the Master* ❧

Lord Jesus, I love John's account of what happened in the Upper Room. You met Thomas where he was at and didn't put him down because he had honest doubts. That gives me the freedom to be honest with my doubts and fears. And Lord, when it finally dawned on Thomas that it was You in the room with him, he fell on his knees and worshiped You. I worship You too, Jesus, because I know You are my Lord and God. In our Lord Jesus' Name. Amen.

FOR LEADERS

(Notes and suggested answers for selected questions.)

ANOTHER LOOK

1. Those in the synagogue looked for a way to have Jesus murdered.

2. Tax collectors were the most despised people in all Israel. They were more worthy of scorn than the Roman soldiers who occupied the Jews' land. In the words of the author, "Most were despicable, vile, unprincipled scoundrels" (p. 152).

3. Since tax collectors were considered traitors to their nation, they would have been considered social and religious outcasts as were the criminals and prostitutes. Similar people (or at least similarly outcast people) hung together.

4. Eeyore, the pessimistic donkey.

5. The appearance of Jesus was beyond Thomas's wildest expectations. The presence of the Savior transformed this previously pessimistic disciple into a great evangelist.

BIBLICAL CONNECTIONS

6. Those in attendance the day Jesus read this prophecy of Isaiah not only took exception that He was implying that He was the Messiah, they also felt He was implying that they were blind, oppressed, and imprisoned by their spiritual ignorance.

7. Each of these passages calls attention to the fact that God exalts the humble and lays low those who are proud.

8. Each one of the tax collectors specifically mentioned received forgiveness. They responded positively to the message Jesus declared.

9. Jesus loved Lazarus and his family, but when He heard Lazarus was dying, He stayed put.

10. In each verse the disciples were not prone to believe at first blush that Jesus was alive. This apprehension to accept the unthinkable is only natural and should serve to comfort us when we find faith a challenge.

11. Matthew was so overwhelmed with joy when he was accepted (and forgiven) by Jesus that he looked for a tangible way to express his happiness. He threw a party at his home.

12. He invited those who were part of his circle of friendship. It appears from this scenario that when Jesus enters a person's life, some kind of response is required. And what is more, that response would naturally include those with whom you share the most in common.

13. Obviously knowledgeable of the Scriptures (self-taught no doubt), he was also obviously morally bankrupt and sick of the life he led. He was only too ready to have the opportunity to start over again.

14. Even though Thomas was convinced that the worst lay ahead, he was willing to lay down his life as a loyal follower of Jesus to embrace that dreadful future. As the author says, "It's not easy to be a pessimist" (p. 160). Still you have to admire Thomas for sensing what was around the corner but still choosing to stay with the plan. It was an indicator of raw courage, but also love for and belief in Jesus.

15. A melancholy personality would be deeply impacted by Jesus' death. His love of the Savior was unquestioned even if he had a pessimistic orientation toward life. He was hurting big time. Curiously, when Jesus invites Thomas to see and touch His wounds, we realize that Jesus wasn't physically present when the "doubting" disciple voiced his reservations. Nonetheless, Jesus was aware of what was said. In addition to His omniscience, Jesus is the epitome of unconditional non-judgmental love. He doesn't put Thomas down for his questions. Instead, He holds out His scarred hands.

DAILY ASSIGNMENTS

Encourage the group participants not only to read the chapter in *Twelve Ordinary Men* assigned for the next lesson (chapter 9), but to use the Daily Assignments to review and remember the truth from God's Word you have just discussed.

James (the Less), Simon (the Zealot), and Judas
(son of James): The Not-So-Well-Known Trio

BIBLICAL FOCUS

Key passages from this section of the book: Luke 18:28; John 6:14–16, 32–68; 14:21–24; Hebrews 11:33–38.

READING ASSIGNMENT

Read chapter 9 of *Twelve Ordinary Men.*

ANOTHER LOOK

The following questions will help you review the material you read in the book.

1. According to MacArthur, "It must be borne in mind that the apostles were men who gave up everything to follow Christ. . . . They had left houses, jobs, lands, family, and friends to follow Christ. Their sacrifice was heroic." Yet he adds, "We don't actually see much of their heroism in the Gospel records" (p. 167). What explanation does he give for this?

   _____

   _____

   _____

   _____

2. On page 168 the author writes, "The Gospel records simply do not portray these men as heroes. Their heroism played out after Jesus went back to heaven, sent the Holy Spirit, and empowered them." How does MacArthur describe their actions in the aftermath of Pentecost?

   _____

   _____

   _____

   _____

3. Besides the two men named James who were part of the Twelve, MacArthur observes, "There are several men with the name *James* in the New Testament" (p. 171). One of the "others" MacArthur describes in some detail became the leader of the Jerusalem church and wrote the small epistle near the end of the New Testament. What is particularly interesting about this James?

   _____

_____

_____

_____

_____

4. MacArthur lists four basic divisions of the Jews that existed in the first century (p. 175). Briefly describe each of them.

- Pharisees

_____

_____

- Sadducees

_____

_____

- Essenes

_____

_____

- Zealots

_____

_____

5. The author points out that the traditional apostolic symbol of Judas Lebbaeus Thaddaeus is a club (p. 180). Explain why this symbol could be both appropriate and ironic.

_____

_____

_____

_____

> ℘ The apostles are not presented to us as mythic figures, but as real people. They are not depicted as prominent celebrities, but as ordinary men. That is why, as far as the Gospel accounts are concerned, the apostles give color and life to the descriptions of Jesus' life, but they are rarely in the foreground. They are never major role players.
>
> When they do come to the foreground, it is often to manifest doubt, disbelief, or confusion. Sometimes we see them thinking more highly of themselves than they ought to think. Sometimes they speak when they ought to remain silent and seem clueless about things they ought to have understood. Sometimes they exhibit more confidence in their own abilities and their own strengths than they should. So their shortcomings and weaknesses show up more often than their strengths. In that sense, the raw honesty of the Gospel accounts is amazing.
>
> —*Twelve Ordinary Men*, p. 168

These questions will allow you to think through the biblical passages John MacArthur uses in this particular lesson.

6. Read John 6:43–71. Based on what Jesus taught in this passage, many turned away from Him. What appears to have been the cause of this desertion? Why didn't the Twelve abandon Him as well?

_____

_____

_____

_____

7. In Hebrews 11:32–38 we find references to anonymous heroes of the faith. The majority of the apostles would find company with these "no-names" because they are not described in the Gospels in detail. After reading over the passage in Hebrews, explain why James the Less, Simon the Zealot, and Judas (not Iscariot) were not given celebrity status in spite of their heroic faithfulness to Jesus.

_____

_____

_____

_____

8. Read Acts 5:20–40. Here Gamaliel, speaking to the Sanhedrin, calls for caution in evaluating the apostles' behavior. He makes reference to the founder of the Zealots. How is the reliability of Scripture underscored by reference to verifiable historical events? In what way does the plight of Judas the Galilean validate Jesus' words in Matthew 26:52?

_____

_____

_____

_____

9. The only words we hear from the lips of Judas Lebbaeus Thaddaeus are in a conversation he had with Jesus recorded in John 14:21–23. Explain the logic of his question as well as the logic of Jesus' answer.

_____

_____

_____

_____

10. What about the question that Judas (not Iscariot) asked Jesus is consistent with Judas's nicknames?

_____

_____

_____

_____

WORD FOCUS

The Greek word for "Less" is *mikros*. It literally means "little." Its primary meaning is "small in stature," so it could refer to his physical features. Perhaps he was a short or small-framed man.

The word can also speak of someone who is young in age. He might have been younger than James the son of Zebedee, so that this title would distinguish him as the younger of the two. In fact, even if this is not what his nickname mainly referred to, it is probably true that he was younger than the other James; otherwise he would more likely have been known as "James the Elder."

But the name most likely refers to his influence. As we have already seen, James the son of Zebedee was a man of prominence. His family was known to the high priest (John 18:15–16). He was part of the Lord's most intimate inner circle. He was the better-known of the two Jameses. Therefore, James the son of Alphaeus was known as "James the Less." *Mikros*. "Little James."

HIGHLIGHTING THE LESSON

These questions have been designed to help you identify the central points MacArthur has made in this section of the book.

11. In the first sidebar (see above), MacArthur makes reference to the fact that we see the apostles' shortcomings and weaknesses more than we do their strengths. Other than underscoring the reliability of the Scriptures (that is, would a propagandistic life of Christ make His followers look bad?), why would the Gospel writers opt for such raw honesty in the description of the Twelve?

   _____
   _____
   _____

12. In addition to his name (which suggests that he was not so important), the only thing we really know about James the Less is the fact that he was the son of a man named Alphaeus. No wonder MacArthur says the only distinguishing mark of this man was his obscurity. In what way does obscurity promote the biblical virtue of humility? (See 1 Peter 5:6.)

   _____
   _____
   _____
   _____

13. In spite of the lack of recognition James the Less (and many others of the Twelve) received, Jesus was quite clear about the reward they would be due in eternity. Read Mark 10:29-31. How might James's lack of celebrity illustrate "deferred gratification"-yet another biblical virtue?

_____

_____

_____

_____

14. God's sense of humor is evidenced in the fact that Matthew (a tax collector who worked for the Romans) and Simon (a Zealot who hated the Romans) were both selected by Jesus to be disciples. How did this unlikely scenario promote the kind of tolerance and cooperation God desires among those in His church?

_____

_____

_____

_____

15. In the following sidebar we see how the names associated with Judas (not Iscariot) actually reveal more to us about who he was than any direct reference of Scripture. It appears that Jesus chose a "tender" man to soften the rough edges that hardheaded individuals like Peter, James, and John brought to the group. What would Judas have learned from those who were unlike him?

_____

_____

_____

_____

> Judas the son of James actually had three names. (Jerome referred to him as "Trinomious"—the man with three names.) In Matthew 10:3, he is called "Lebbaeus, whose surname was Thaddaeus." *Judas* was probably the name given him at birth. *Lebbaeus* and *Thaddaeus* were essentially nicknames. *Thaddaeus* means "breast child"—evoking the idea of a nursing baby. It almost has a derisive sound, like "mamma's boy." Perhaps he was the youngest in his family, and therefore the baby among several siblings—specially cherished by his mother. His other name, *Lebbaeus*, is similar. It is from a Hebrew root that refers to the heart—literally "heart child."
>
> —*Twelve Ordinary Men*, p. 178

LASTING IMPLICATIONS

The following questions will assist you in drawing personal application from God's Word.

16. MacArthur says, "If the faults and character flaws of the apostles seem like a mirror of your own weaknesses, take heart. These are the kinds of people the Lord delights to use" (p. 169). In light of that, why shouldn't Christians disqualify themselves from service opportunities for which they feel inadequate?

_____

_____

_____

_____

17. Simon the Zealot was known by his nickname all his life; therefore, we can assume that he remained passionate and zealous. Whom do you know at church whose personality and experience the Lord utilized for the kingdom after that person became a Christian? How does that example prompt you to look at your unique skills?

_____

_____

_____

_____

18. Amazingly, the Zealots' hatred and bloodshed was the indirect cause of Jerusalem being destroyed. Their unrestrained passion undermined the goal that motivated them. What lessons can be learned from this in terms of the passions that fill people's hearts today?

_____

_____

_____

_____

19. Among the Twelve, MacArthur suggests, we see one of almost every imaginable personality type. Why did Jesus opt for that kind of diversity?

_____

_____

_____

_____

20. In spite of the obscurity in the Gospels that characterizes James the Less, Simon the Zealot, and Judas (not Iscariot), Jesus affirmed and included them in His mission. How does God feel about the people in your congregation who work behind the scenes without much public recognition?

_____

_____

_____

_____

> The Zealots were extremists in every sense. Like the Pharisees, they interpreted the Law literally. Unlike the Pharisees (who were willing to compromise for political reasons) the Zealots were militant, violent outlaws. They believed only God Himself had the right to rule over the Jews. And therefore they believed they were doing God's work by assassinating Roman soldiers, political leaders, and anyone else who opposed them.
>
> —*Twelve Ordinary Men, p. 175*

DAILY ASSIGNMENTS

MONDAY

Read Luke 18:28–30.

1. How does Peter choose to call attention to the sacrifice he has made to follow Jesus?

_____

_____

_____

_____

2. In these verses, what indicates Peter's frustration?

_____

_____

_____

_____

3. How does Jesus respond to Peter's statement?

_____

_____

_____

_____

4. What did Jesus mean by His own declaration?

_____

_____

_____

_____

5. In what ways have you found Jesus' statement to be true since you have been following Him?

_____

_____

_____

_____

6. When are you most apt to be aware of the price tag associated with being a committed Christian?

_____

_____

_____

_____

7. In light of the sacrifices the apostles made, why do you think Christians are so quick to complain about inconvenience or sacrifice?

_____

_____

_____

_____

✑ *Imitating the Master* ✑

Lord, I'm a bit ashamed of the way I complain so much of the time. Compared to the Twelve, I haven't even begun to know the meaning of sacrifice. When You do call me to be more like them by giving up things I treasure, help me to respond obediently and optimistically. Remind me that the same reward You promised the Twelve awaits all who lay down their lives for You. In our Lord Jesus' Name. Amen.

Tuesday

Read John 6:53–71.

1. What did Jesus say that many of the disciples found hard to accept or understand?

_____

_____

_____

_____

2. How was Jesus feeling as He looked over the dwindling crowd of people? Why?

_____

_____

_____

_____

3. What question did He ask the Twelve?

_____

_____

_____

_____

4. How would you have felt if you had witnessed this scene?

_____
_____
_____
_____

5. Why is Peter's answer so significant?

_____
_____
_____
_____

6. In spite of the mysterious words Peter hears but cannot fully understand, he detects that he is in the presence of God. Have you ever felt that way? When?

_____
_____
_____
_____

7. Why did John include Jesus' statement that even among the Twelve, one would turn out to be "a devil"?

_____
_____
_____
_____

✑ *Imitating the Master* ✑

Jesus, I can almost hear the sadness in Your voice as You asked Your closest followers if they were going to leave You like the others. I'm sure You are grieved when my actions are not consistent with my faith. Forgive me, Lord. With Peter, I can't imagine any place I'd rather be than with You. I love You and I need You. Empower me to express my gratitude for all You've done for me by the way that I speak and act today. In our Lord Jesus' Name. Amen.

Wednesday

Read Hebrews 11:32–40.

1. What evidences of God's power in human lives is illustrated in these verses?

_____
_____
_____
_____

2. What specific tribulations did these faithful ones experience?

_____

_____

_____

_____

3. Explain the meaning of the phrase "of whom the world was not worthy."

_____

_____

_____

_____

4. In what ways are individuals persecuted for their faith today?

_____

_____

_____

_____

5. How would the phrase "out of weakness were made strong" be appropriate for those who experience hardship as they live out their faith?

_____

_____

_____

_____

6. How do the experiences of these real saints compare with typical expectations of blessings and the good life that seem to be the expectations of some believers today?

_____

_____

_____

_____

7. In what ways, according to the author of Hebrews, do we actually benefit from the suffering of those Old Testament saints?

_____

_____

_____

_____

❧ *Imitating the Master* ❧

Lord, I long for that to be said of me. "The world was not worthy of the kind of courageous suffering he/she endured for the sake of Christ." Like the faithful disciples and the unnamed heroes in Hebrews 11, I want my life to count even if I'm added to the list of obscure unknown saints in the shadows. To that end, I need to keep short accounts with You. In our Lord Jesus' Name. Amen.

Read John 19:17–27.

1. Who was standing at the foot of the cross witnessing Jesus' death?

_____

_____

_____

_____

2. Compare this reference to Mark 15:40. Why do some think that one of the Marys at the crucifixion was the mother of the disciple called James the Less?

_____

_____

_____

_____

3. What aspects of Jesus' ministry did each of those women represent?

_____

_____

_____

_____

4. Apart from whether this is the mother of the disciple or if James the Less was Jesus' first cousin, what do you find significant about the fact that Jesus' mother was not alone in her grief?

_____

_____

_____

_____

5. Jesus obviously desired others to share in His ministry even as Mary needed someone to stand with her in His death. How is the principle of "power in community" still applicable today?

_____

_____

_____

_____

6. What can we learn from the fact that Jesus drew comfort and strength from people like James, Simon, and Judas whose background was left sketchy?

_____

_____

_____

_____

7. Who are the people in your life that you know you can count on through thick and thin? Express your thanksgiving to God for them as you jot down their names.

_____

_____

_____

_____

∞ *Imitating the Master* ∞

Jesus, I need others in my life to live the kind of life You desire of me. Lone Ranger Christianity is an oxymoron. Even the masked man on the white horse had a Tonto. Give me the courage to open up with others about the issues in my life that I tend to cover up or deal with alone. In our Lord Jesus' Name. Amen.

FRIDAY

Read John 14:21–24.

1. According to Jesus, how does a person validate his or her verbalized love for Him?

_____

_____

_____

_____

2. How does this insistence by Jesus go against the primary dogma of our culture that love is about feelings?

_____

_____

_____

_____

3. How does Jesus say He will reward the person who values God's Word and seeks to live according to it?

_____

_____

_____

_____

4. The picture of Jesus making His home with the faithful follower is a vivid one. Compare it to what you find in Revelation 3:20.

_____

_____

_____

_____

5. What does Jesus' "taking up residence in our lives" mean in a practical sense?

_____
_____
_____
_____

6. Judas is mind-boggled and humbled by the thought that Jesus would manifest His glory to him (and the other apostles). How does one go about maintaining a sense of "awe" when it comes to acknowledging God's mercy in our lives?

_____
_____
_____
_____

7. When was the last time you experienced awe over all that God has done in your life?

_____
_____
_____
_____

❧ Imitating the Master ❧

Lord Jesus, I never want to get used to the fact that You have sought me out and called me to be a follower of Yours. The fact that Judas (not Iscariot) was mystified that You manifested Yourself to him is something I can't let go of. I am convicted by his sensitivity. He didn't feel worthy, and yet too often I take Your blessings in my life for granted. Forgive me, Lord. In our Lord Jesus' Name.
Amen.

FOR LEADERS

(Notes and suggested answers for selected questions.)

ANOTHER LOOK

1. The Gospel writers wanted the essence of their story to be about Jesus. The references to the apostles provided color and contrast, but the spotlight remained on Jesus. Scripture deliberately records more about Jesus and His teaching than it does about the lives of these men.

2. They are strong and courageous. They perform great miracles. They preach with newfound boldness.

3. This James was the half brother of Jesus (Galatians 1:19).

4. According to Josephus the Jewish historian:
Pharisees—these religious fundamentalists were fastidious about the law.
Sadducees—these rich religious liberals denied the supernatural.
Essenes—these ascetic celibates lived in the desert studying the Law.
Zealots—these terrorists wanted to overthrow the Roman government.

5. Tradition says that Judas was clubbed to death for his faith. For a tender-hearted "mamma's boy," such an end was truly a testament to his devotion and courage.

BIBLICAL CONNECTIONS

6. Jesus taught what seemed to some to be cannibalism. To others it was clear that He was equating Himself with God (like "manna from heaven"). In either case, most were offended. But the disciples did not bail out because they understood enough of the veiled language to sense that Jesus was their only hope. They were courageous to be sure. But Jesus also makes reference in John 6:44 that the Father was involved in drawing to Him those who would remain.

7. They were not the only ones who suffered for their faith. In fact, "saints in the shadows" is the norm in the Scriptures.

8. When events of secular history are mentioned in Scripture, the accuracy of the Bible in the minds of nonbelievers is elevated. Judas the Galilean was wiped out (along with the other Zealots) because violence ends in a violent way. No wonder Jesus taught the concept of forgiveness and turning the other cheek.

9. It would be only natural for Judas to wonder why he and his friends were being given the opportunity to encounter the Messiah. Who were they to deserve such an honor? Who indeed! Jesus explains that His approach with them (a nonmilitaristic kingdom) is accessible to all who open their hearts to Him.

10. Unlike brash Peter who challenges Jesus, or James and John who boldly ask for favors, Judas the tenderhearted gentle man quietly asks a question that isn't an affront to anybody. And Jesus graciously answered him in kind.

11 It is an intentional ploy on their part to remind us that Jesus is pleased to use imperfect people in His mission. Reading about these men allows us to identify with them more than we would with superheroes.

12. From James's point of view, if you aren't in the spotlight, you don't have to deal with ego as much. From our point of view, the lack of description or adulation helps us see that God uses humble servants who aren't "in it" for the glory. As we humble ourselves (and do not seek attention), we can be assured that God has a place for us. On the other hand, if we struggle with issues of ego or pride, the lack of details associated with the disciples shows us how easy it is for God to humble us by deleting "pertinent" information.

13. James was not concerned about being remembered in a book Matthew or John would write about their exploits as disciples. He was most concerned with what Jesus had promised. He understood that waiting for ultimate rewards and recognition was far more important than seeking short-lived pleasure or popularity in this life.

14. Jesus desires us to learn to get along with and appreciate those who come at life differently than we do. This is a wonderful example of "bearing with one another" (Colossians 3:13).

15. Judas was a gift to the group. They were a gift to him. His soft-spoken, gentle personality helped the group mellow out. The outspoken extroverts helped Judas know how to speak up and be assertive. As Paul suggests in 1 Corinthians 12, every part of the body is important and contributes to helping the other parts function.

DAILY ASSIGNMENTS

Encourage the group participants not only to read the chapter in *Twelve Ordinary Men* assigned for the next lesson (chapter 10), but to use the Daily Assignments to review and remember the truth from God's Word you have just discussed.

Judas: The Devil's Disciple

BIBLICAL FOCUS

Key passages from this section of the book: Psalm 41:9; 55:12–14; Zechariah 11:12–13; Matthew 6:19–34; 22:11–14; 23:1–12; 27:3–8; Luke 13:13–21; John 12:1–11, 23–30; 13:8, 18–30.

READING ASSIGNMENT

Read chapter 10 of *Twelve Ordinary Men*.

ANOTHER LOOK

The following questions will help you review the material you read in the book.

1. According to the author, it was easy for Judas Iscariot to play the hypocrite. What contributed most to that?

   _____
   _____
   _____
   _____

2. MacArthur claims that Judas never was drawn to the Person of Christ. What does he suggest was Judas's goal in spending time with Jesus?

   _____
   _____
   _____
   _____

3. MacArthur writes, "Judas did not act in a moment of insanity. This was not a sudden impulse. It was not an act borne only out of passion. This dark deed was deliberately planned and premeditated. He had been planning this for days, if not weeks or even months" (p. 193). What does MacArthur offer as the most obvious proof that this was the case?

   _____
   _____
   _____
   _____

4. From the start, the Twelve believed that Jesus was the fulfillment of the Old Testament prophecies. But their understanding of how that would play out was more political than spiritual. According to the author, "The rest of the disciples had begun to catch on slowly that the true Messiah was not what they at first expected. They embraced the superior understanding of the biblical promises Jesus unfolded to them" (p. 187). But how did Judas deal with the redefined role of the Messiah that Jesus offered?

_____

_____

_____

_____

5. While some have struggled over an apparent contradiction in details about Judas and the Field of Blood (Matthew 27:6-8; Acts 1:18–19), the author thinks such a struggle unnecessary. He writes that, "all apparent discrepancies are easily reconciled" (p. 196). How so?

_____

_____

_____

_____

> Judas was as common as the rest, without earthly credentials and without any characteristics that made him stand out from the group. He began exactly like the others had begun. But he never laid hold of the truth by faith, so he was never transformed like the rest. While they were increasing in faith as sons of God, he was becoming more and more a child of hell.
>
> —*Twelve Ordinary Men, p. 182*

BIBLICAL CONNECTIONS

These questions will allow you to think through the biblical passages John MacArthur uses in this particular lesson.

6. Judas's dark deed was predicted centuries before. In John 13:18, Jesus calls attention to the fact that He is about to be betrayed and cites Psalm 41:9 as a reference point. Beginning with that passage, describe how each Old Testament Scripture relates to Jesus and Judas.
Psalm 41:9

_____

_____

Psalm 55:12–14

_____

Zechariah 11:12–13

_____

_____

7. In Genesis 50:20 Joseph reflects on the injustices he has personally endured that were instigated by the sinful motives of his brothers. After looking up that verse, what correlation do you see between Joseph's experience at the hands of his siblings and Jesus' experience at the hands of Judas?

_____

_____

_____

_____

8. "Judas had every opportunity to turn from his sin," the author asserts on page 186. What should he have gleaned from the following lessons he heard Jesus give?
   Matthew 6:19–34

_____

_____

   Matthew 22:11–14

_____

_____

   Matthew 23:1–12

_____

_____

   Luke 13:13–21

_____

_____

   Luke 16:1–13

_____

_____

9. Read the poignant story in John 12:1–11. Apparently the "wasted" ointment and Jesus' response to Judas were the turning point in the traitor that began his process of betrayal. What contrast can you detect in the attitudes and actions between the woman who anoints Jesus and the man who betrays Him? Does anything in this scene surprise you?

_____

_____

_____

_____

10. In Matthew 27:3–5, we peek into the turbulent heart of Judas after he sees that Jesus has been condemned to die. Would you describe Judas as repentant or remorseful? Why?

_____

_____

_____

_____

 WORD FOCUS

Judas's name is a form of *Judah.* The name means "Jehovah leads," which indicates that when he was born his parents must have had great hopes for him to be led by God. The irony of the name is that no individual was ever more clearly led by Satan than Judas was.

His surname, *Iscariot,* signified the region he came from. It is derived from the Hebrew term *ish* ("man") and the name of a town, Kerioth— "man of Kerioth." Judas probably came from Kerioth-hezron (cf. Joshua 15:25), a humble town in the south of Judea. He was apparently the only one of the apostles who did not come from Galilee. As we know, many of the others were brothers, friends, and working companions even before meeting Christ. Judas was a solitary figure who entered their midst from afar.

—*Twelve Ordinary Men, pp. 182–183*

HIGHLIGHTING THE LESSON

These questions have been designed to help you identify the central points MacArthur has made in this section of the book.

11. Although Scripture had predicted that Judas would betray Jesus, he was in no way coerced into this act of ultimate shame. It is clear that Judas entertained greed, ambition, and wicked desires in his heart even though he was viewed as one of Jesus' followers and had every advantage of the other eleven disciples. How do you explain this irony?

_____

_____

_____

_____

12. Which of the following bumper sticker slogans best captures the nineteenth-century British preacher Charles Spurgeon's attempt to make sense of God's sovereignty and the free will of the individual? Why? (Circle one and then explain using the lines provided on the following page)
    • Who said puppets have to be made of wood?
    • If God said it's true but it seems false to you, guess who's goofy?
    • For heaven's sake, you're both right!
    • God goes first in the game of life. (He's really the only player).

_____
_____
_____
_____

> ℮ The New Testament tells us plenty about Judas—enough to accomplish two things: First, the life of Judas reminds us that it is possible to be near Christ and associate with Him closely (but superficially) and yet become utterly hardened in sin. Second, Judas reminds us that no matter how sinful a person may be, no matter what treachery he or she may attempt against God, the purpose of God cannot be thwarted. Even the worst act of treachery works toward the fulfillment of the divine plan. God's sovereign plan cannot be overthrown even by the most cunning schemes of those who hate Him.
>
> —*Twelve Ordinary Men, p. 182*

13. In the above sidebar, the author draws two conclusions from the tragic life of Judas. Which of these two lessons is illustrated in the following biblical personalities? What warnings or encouragement does each person's story offer the Christian?

    • King Saul

    _____
    _____

    • Joseph

    _____
    _____

    • Solomon

    _____
    _____

    • Stephen

    _____
    _____

LASTING IMPLICATIONS

The following questions will assist you in drawing personal conclusions from God's Word. They are drawn from the seven lessons from the life of Judas that the author mentions on pages 197–198.

14. In spite of the rare opportunity Judas had to learn from or receive help from the Lord, Judas didn't take advantage of these one-on-one settings. What

opportunities for personal growth are available to the people of God that we often ignore?

_____

_____

_____

_____

15. Judas had the enviable privilege of being one of the Twelve, yet he cashed in this priceless honor for thirty pieces of silver. What privileges does the Lord guarantee those who enter into a personal relationship with Him that are easily squandered without thought of their worth?

_____

_____

_____

_____

16. Judas went down in history as living (and dying) proof that the love of money is the root of all kinds of evil. From what you have observed, how does a preoccupation with material things suck the energy and blur the focus of Christians in today's culture?

_____

_____

_____

_____

17. Judas is proof of the patient, forbearing goodness of Jesus. The Lord's unconditional love never wavered toward the traitor. He called him a friend to the very end. If you truly believed that there is nothing you could ever do that would cause you to earn (or lose) God's favor, what impact would it have on the way you respond to what His Word requires?

_____

_____

_____

_____

18. Although Judas's life of deception and his ultimate act of betrayal played into Satan's plan to destroy him and humiliate Christ, God's sovereign plan for His creation was not undermined in the least. How does God's ultimate control in this scenario (in which Judas facilitated His Son's being mocked and killed) challenge the way you look at "bad news" in the world?

_____

_____

_____

_____

19. Judas is proof of the fact that hypocrisy is lethal. If not confessed and turned from, it separates a person increasingly from the truth. Although it is easy to

cover up, it eventually comes to light. Since it has soul-damaging consequences, what steps should a person take to root out the initial growth of hypocrisy?

_____

_____

_____

_____

> ℭ From a human perspective, Judas had the same potential as the others. The difference is that he was never really drawn to the Person of Christ. He saw Him only as a means to an end. Judas's secret goal was personal prosperity—gain for himself. He never embraced Jesus' teaching by faith. He never had an ounce of true love for Christ. His heart had never been changed, and therefore the light of truth only hardened him.
>
> —*Twelve Ordinary Men, p. 186*

DAILY ASSIGNMENTS

MONDAY

Read Ephesians 1:1–11.

1. How do these verses support the view that God is never surprised by what happens in our lives?

   _____

   _____

   _____

   _____

2. What other highlights do you see in this section of Scripture?

   _____

   _____

   _____

   _____

3. What, according to this passage, does God's predestined plan include?

   _____

   _____

   _____

   _____

4. What in this passage suggests the kind of privileges Judas had as a member of the Twelve?

   _____

   _____

   _____

   _____

5. When you contemplate that you were chosen by God to be part of His forever family before the world was even created, what thoughts or feelings do you have?

_____

_____

_____

_____

6. If God is committed to working everything out according to His purposes, does that free Christians to be careless in their lives? Why or why not?

_____

_____

_____

_____

7. Describe your highest sense of responsibility within God's purposes for your life (review pages 185–186).

_____

_____

_____

_____

❧ *Imitating the Master* ❧

Lord, I can't say I even begin to understand how my choices and Your choices can co-exist. But based on those wonderful verses in the first chapter of Ephesians, the apostle Paul found reason to celebrate the fact that it is true. I want to celebrate it, too. Help me remember when I think that "it all depends on me," that You are really in control and that I belong to You. In our Lord Jesus' Name. Amen.

TUESDAY

Read Matthew 6:19–34.

1. What risks are taken by those who store up treasures on earth?

_____

_____

_____

_____

2. What alternative to earthly riches does Jesus pose?

_____

_____

_____

_____

3. When Jesus spoke about the location of the heart being near the treasure, what was He indicating would happen to the person who chooses the wrong treasure?

_____
_____
_____
_____

4. How did Judas's love of money result in "destruction"?

_____
_____
_____
_____

5. What about our culture allows a person who is really serving Money to appear as though he is serving God?

_____
_____
_____
_____

6. What might Judas have been thinking when he heard the words recorded in this passage fall from Jesus' lips?

_____
_____
_____
_____

7. Describe your treasure.

_____
_____
_____
_____

❧ *Imitating the Master* ❧

Jesus, it's so obvious to me that Judas was motivated by personal gain. I confess that such is true for me too much of the time. It's not Money as much as it is me that I am tempted to worship. But that's just as dangerous. I need Your help to keep my eyes off my personal goals and on Yours. I don't want to grieve You with the foolish choices I'm tempted to make. Today, I confess _____. Keep me clean, Lord. Keep my strong. In our Lord Jesus' Name. Amen.

WEDNESDAY

Read John 12:1–11.

1. What appeared to trouble Judas about the way the fragrant oil was used?

_____

_____

_____

_____

2. Why didn't Jesus share Judas's indignation?

_____

_____

_____

_____

3. As best as you can tell, what motivated Mary's action?

_____

_____

_____

_____

4. What is the most extravagant gift (that you're aware of) that has been given to the Lord's work?

_____

_____

_____

_____

5. In what way have you chosen to express your deepest appreciation for all that Christ has done for you?

_____

_____

_____

_____

6. Why is it easy to cover up personal greed by diverting attention away from your own values, as Judas did on this occasion?

_____

_____

_____

_____

7. Based on His response to Mary's gift, how does Jesus recognize sacrificial gifts from those who love Him?

_____

_____

_____

Lord, the extravagance of Mary's gift humbles me—a year's worth of income spent on an expression of devotion. I can't imagine doing that, and that's troubling to me that I can't. There's a bit of Judas in me after all. Instead of bowing at Your feet, I'm looking at the bottom line. Forgive me, Jesus. Remind me how to give myself away to You (as well as to others). In our Lord Jesus' Name. Amen.

THURSDAY

Read John 13:21–30.

1. What about this passage makes it clear that the disciples didn't know the identity of Jesus' betrayer?

   _____

   _____

   _____

   _____

2. What clue is contained in these verses that Judas had a fascination with money?

   _____

   _____

   _____

   _____

3. Describe the main differences between having money and money having you.

   _____

   _____

   _____

   _____

4. Why is John's use of the word "night" quite possibly more than an indication that it was after sundown?

   _____

   _____

   _____

   _____

5. Does your lack of insight into the true spiritual condition of the people with whom you worship prevent you from fully worshiping the Lord? Why or why not?

   _____

   _____

   _____

   _____

6. No doubt all the individuals in the Upper Room began to conduct an internal inventory as they questioned Jesus about who was the guilty one. Since every one of the disciples abandoned Jesus within hours of these moments, what do you think they found when they made their personal inventories?

_____

_____

_____

_____

7. How often do you think a person should look into his or her heart for wrong motives? Explain.

_____

_____

_____

_____

❧ *Imitating the Master* ❧

Jesus, even though this passage indicates that Judas had successfully fooled the others (because they didn't know he was the betrayer), each wondered who the betrayer was. There's something about that ignorance that's refreshing to me. They were willing to accept whatever You said was true whether they felt guilty or not. As I come to You in a moment of silence, would You point out anything in my heart that grieves You? My desire is to confess it and accept Your forgiveness. In our Lord Jesus' Name. Amen.

FRIDAY

Read John 15:1–10.

1. To what does Jesus compare a person's relationship with Him?

_____

_____

_____

_____

2. According to Jesus' figurative language, whose responsibility is it to produce fruit—the vine or the branch?

_____

_____

_____

_____

3. What do you find helpful about this description of your relationship with Christ?

_____

_____

_____

_____

4. Based on the context, what does Jesus mean by "abiding" in the vine?

_____

_____

_____

_____

5. Why didn't Judas bear fruit?

_____

_____

_____

_____

6. From those whom you've observed who have borne much fruit, what choices and disciplines have they made to "abide in" the vine?

_____

_____

_____

_____

7. What fosters the clearest sense in your life that you are "abiding" in Christ?

_____

_____

_____

_____

❧ Imitating the Master ❧

Lord Jesus, the vine and branches metaphor is a graphic one. It's also a reassuring one. I'm grateful, Jesus, that my primary task is to stay connected to You rather than trying to produce fruit on my own. You are the life and You bring the fruit into being. Thank You for the life that You have given me.
In our Lord Jesus' Name. Amen.

FOR LEADERS

(Notes and suggested answers for selected questions.)

ANOTHER LOOK

1. Judas was from a humble town south of Jerusalem. The others, who were from Galilee, knew nothing about his family or his background before Judas joined them. Thus, the betrayer was able to work his way into a place of trust without being suspected.

2. Judas was only after personal prosperity.

3. He had already taken the money for it (Matthew 26:15).

4. He grew increasingly disillusioned but hid his jaded response from the others by hypocritically pretending to go along with the program.

5. While the Matthew account indicates that the chief priests bought the field and Acts implies that Judas bought it, both are right. It was Judas's money that the priests used after his suicide to buy the land.

BIBLICAL CONNECTIONS

6 The passages relate as follows:
Psalm 41:9—At the Last Supper, Judas broke bread with Jesus before lifting up "his heel" against Him.
Psalm 55:12–14—Judas was one of Jesus' closest friends. For over three years they had traveled, worshiped, and ministered together.
Zechariah 11:12–13—Judas agreed to sell Jesus to the religious leaders for thirty pieces of silver. He then threw the blood money into the temple, but it was eventually used to buy a plot of land.

7. In both cases God incorporated the evil schemes of sinful men into His perfect plan of redemption (in Joseph's case the redemption of Israel).

8. Judas should have identified himself:
Matthew 16:19–34—As one who was laying up treasure on earth
Matthew 22:11–14—As the man who did not have on a wedding garment
Matthew 23:1–12—As one who was guilty of pride
Luke 13:13–21—As one who had a faulty perception of Christ's kingdom
Luke 16:1–13—As the unjust servant

9. The woman is totally transparent. She holds nothing back in her expression of extravagant love. Judas is the picture of hypocrisy. He is anything but transparent. He pretends to have concern for the poor. He moves from this scene to set in motion a plot that is nothing less than extravagant hate.

HIGHLIGHTING THE LESSON

13. Saul and Solomon both proved that exposure to the truth of God is not sufficient to persevere in a faithful life. Christians should be warned that simply being with other Christians does not guarantee growth. Joseph and Stephen prove that when evil appears to triumph, God is nonetheless working His perfect plan. Their lives encourage Christians to trust God even when it appears as though He has abandoned them.

Encourage the group to review the book *Twelve Ordinary Men* next week and use the Daily Assignments to review and remember the truth from God's Word you have just discussed.

Looking Back, Looking Forward

BIBLICAL FOCUS

Key passages from the book: Matthew 10:1–4; Mark 3:13–14; Luke 5:17–6:16; 1 Corinthians 1:26–29; 1 Timothy 3:2–7.

READING ASSIGNMENT

Review all ten chapters of *Twelve Ordinary Men.*

ANOTHER LOOK

The following questions will help you review the material you read in the book.

1. What does the author state to be the reason Jesus didn't include a rabbi or anyone who represented the Jewish religious establishment to be part of His inner circle?

   _____

   _____

   _____

   _____

2. Jesus didn't actually choose these twelve as apostles until His earthly ministry was half over. What observations did the author draw from this often-overlooked detail?

   _____

   _____

   _____

   _____

3. What kinds of occupations did the apostles represent, and what part of Israel did they come from?

   _____

   _____

   _____

   _____

4. What did the author suggest could be gleaned from the order in which the apostles' names are listed in the Gospels?

_____

_____

_____

_____

5. Note some examples of ways in which Jesus used nicknames for His disciples in challenging and affirming ways.

_____

_____

_____

> ℘ And when He had called His twelve disciples to Him, He gave them power over unclean spirits, to cast them out, and to heal all kinds of sickness and all kinds of disease. Now the names of the twelve apostles are these: first, Simon, who is called Peter, and Andrew his brother; James the son of Zebedee, and John his brother; Philip and Bartholomew; Thomas and Matthew the tax collector; James the son of Alphaeus, and Lebbaeus, whose surname was Thaddaeus; Simon the Cananite, and Judas Iscariot, who also betrayed Him.
>
> —*Matthew 10:1–4*
>
> Jesus delegated His power to the apostles to show clearly that He and His kingdom were sovereign over the physical and spiritual realms, the effects of sin, and the efforts of Satan. This was an unheard of display of power, never before seen in all redemptive history, to announce Messiah's arrival and authenticate Him plus His apostles who preached His gospel.
>
> —*John MacArthur*[2]

BIBLICAL CONNECTIONS

These questions will allow you to think through some of the biblical passages John MacArthur uses in the book.

6. In 1 Corinthians 1:26–29, we find the key passage that supports the title of MacArthur's book. What does the apostle Paul assert about those whom God is pleased to use? For what reason?

_____

_____

_____

_____

7. Mark 3:13–19 is but one of several listings of the disciples. What is said about the nature of Jesus' calling of them is unique? What two aspects are there to His call? Is the order of these aspects significant?

_____
_____
_____
_____

8. Read John 12:20–22. This passage of Scripture provides a paradigm of how the church operates as a "body of interrelated parts" in order to fulfill the Great Commission. Do your best to identify the elements of this paradigm.

_____
_____
_____
_____

9. In Romans 7:14–25, the apostle who was not one of the Twelve leaves little doubt that he had much in common with them. What does Paul say about himself that was consistent with the others? How does he describe his frailty? What does he admit is his only hope?

_____
_____
_____
_____

10. Read John 21. What do you learn about Jesus in relationship to:
The disciples

_____
_____

Peter

_____
_____

John

_____
_____

🐟 WORD FOCUS

Gospel: Greek *euangelion*—[Mark] 1:1, 14–15; 13:10; 14:9; 16:15—literally, "good news" or "good message." Messengers bringing news of victory in battle originally used this Greek term. In the New Testament it points to the Good News of salvation: Jesus Christ came to earth to abolish the power of sin in the lives of His people by offering Himself as a perfect sacrifice on the cross. Christ commands believers to share this Good News with the rest of the world. This Good News is Christ's life-giving message to a dying world (16:15).

—*John MacArthur*[3]

HIGHLIGHTING THE LESSON

These questions have been designed to help you identify the central points MacArthur has made throughout the book.

11. What significance does the author attach to the fact that Jesus specifically chose twelve (instead of eight or ten) to be His apostles?

    _____

    _____

    _____

    _____

12. Even though half of the apostles were fishermen and had a previous relationship prior to their call, some of them were quite different from one another. Cite an example of such a pairing and explain what Jesus had in mind by including such opposites in His group of twelve.

    _____

    _____

    _____

    _____

13. How does MacArthur make a case for friendship evangelism? Give an example or two.

    _____

    _____

    _____

    _____

14. Many of those who were called had an impressive knowledge of Scripture before Jesus approached them. What clues did the author provide that illustrated this? How did this prior knowledge serve the "called ones" later on?

    _____

    _____

    _____

    _____

15. All but John and Judas died as martyrs for their faith (and John was exiled to a desolate island as an old man). What do the lives and ultimate deaths of Jesus' apostles suggest about the transforming power of following Christ?

    _____

    _____

    _____

    _____

These studies in the lives of the apostles have been a particular delight for me—and one of the most fruitful endeavors of my life. My greatest Joy is preaching Christ. Eleven of these men shared that passion, devoted their lives to it, and triumphed in it against overwhelming opposition. They are fitting heroes and role models for us, despite their shortcomings. To study their lives is to get to know the men who were closest to Christ during His eartly life. To realize that they were ordinary people just like you and me is a great blessing. May the Spirit of Christ who taught them transform us the way He transformed them, into precious vessels fit for the Master's use. And may we learn from their example what it means to be disciples indeed.

—*Twelve Ordinary Men, p. xviii*

[LASTING IMPLICATIONS

The following questions will assist you in drawing personal conclusions from God's Word.

16. As a result of this study, for which of the apostles have you gained a new appreciation? Explain.

_____
_____
_____
_____

17. Which one of the Twelve did you find yourself relating to the most easily? Why?

_____
_____
_____
_____

18. What conclusions can you draw from the fact that when Jesus called the apostles, He personalized His approach?

_____
_____
_____
_____

19. Were you surprised by the way the apostles demonstrated selfishness, spiritual ignorance, and lack of loyalty even after their lengthy discipleship program? Why or why not?

_____

_____

_____

_____

20. In light of the twelve lives you have encountered in this workbook, what do you sense the Lord calling you to do as one of His disciples?

_____

_____

_____

_____

DAILY ASSIGNMENTS

MONDAY

Read 1 Corinthians 1:26–29.

1. What percentage of the church in Corinth could be described as extraordinarily gifted individuals?

_____

_____

_____

_____

2. What percentage of the Twelve would you say were mighty or noble?

_____

_____

_____

_____

3. How does the message in these verses contrast with the emphasis on self-importance that is so prevalent in society today?

_____

_____

_____

_____

4. MacArthur suggests that Peter was exactly like most Christians—both carnal and spiritual. Can you recall an example of each kind of response in Peter's life?

_____

_____

_____

5. Identify a time in the past month when you succumbed to the habits of the flesh.

_____
_____
_____
_____

6. Describe an occasion when you functioned as a spiritually sensitive follower of Christ.

_____
_____
_____
_____

7. What qualities in Peter's life would you most like to exhibit in your life? Why?

_____
_____
_____
_____

∂ Imitating the Master ∂

Lord, in terms of the way society judges greatness, I'm far from the top. At times I let that get me down. Even though I know that how You measure importance matters more, I succumb to what others think of me more often than I'd like to admit. But I want to live my life for You today as ordinary as I am. Thanks for the reminder of Peter that You can use those who stumble with regularity.
In our Lord Jesus' Name. Amen.

TUESDAY

Read John 1:40–42.

1. What was Andrew's first response when he realized that Jesus was the Lamb of God?

_____
_____
_____
_____

2. How would you describe the most startling discovery you've made about Jesus?

_____
_____
_____

3. What do you make of the phrase "brought him to Jesus"?

_____

_____

_____

_____

4. As you look at members of your family who don't know Jesus, whom do you think you could approach first with an invitation to a ministry event?

_____

_____

_____

_____

5. How many ways could you express gratitude for the fact that someone introduced you to Jesus (beyond passing on the invitation to someone else)?

_____

_____

_____

_____

6. James had a thunderous personality. How was that a personal strength? In what way was it a weakness?

_____

_____

_____

_____

7. As you contemplate the way God wired you, how are your strengths at the same time your weaknesses?

_____

_____

_____

_____

❦ Imitating the Master ❦

Jesus, I am grateful for the abilities and interests I possess. They help me to celebrate my uniqueness. But I also know that what I am good at can also get in Your way. They can be a source of unhealthy pride. They can cause me to take my eyes off You. Forgive me Lord when that happens. Glorify Yourself through me.

In our Lord Jesus' Name. Amen.

Read Mark 9:1–41.

1. What conversations occurred among James, John, and Peter in the aftermath of the Transfiguration?

_____

_____

_____

_____

2. How did Jesus rebuke them?

_____

_____

_____

_____

3. John was apparently convicted about his legalistic attitude toward a group he had put down. Was John confessing in order to be forgiven or to be affirmed?

_____

_____

_____

_____

4. How do people who have experienced the power and effects of God's grace keep from looking down on those around them?

_____

_____

_____

_____

5. If John was "black and white" in the way he looked at life and Philip was "a bean counter," what was Jesus probably saying to them much of the time?

_____

_____

_____

_____

6. In your orientation to life, what is a "black and white/by the book" attitude the Lord might want to challenge?

_____

_____

_____

_____

7. How might God make you aware of such an attitude?

_____

_____

_____

_____

❧ *Imitating the Master* ❧

You know me, Jesus, inside and out. You are aware of how I enjoy my way of doing things. You know I hate it when people disagree with me. But Lord, it is quite possible that I need to be stretched. Bring others into my life this week who will help me evaluate how loving I really am. In our Lord Jesus' Name. Amen.

THURSDAY

Read John 1:43–51.

1. In these verses, what indicates that Nathanael was spiritually sensitive, culturally aware, and personally biased?

_____

_____

_____

_____

2. How did Philip answer Nathanael's reservation?

_____

_____

_____

_____

3. What about Philip's answer is nonthreatening and limits personal risks?

_____

_____

_____

_____

4. If Nathanael had been invited to "come and see" who was at the party Matthew threw for Jesus, who would he have seen?

_____

_____

_____

_____

5. What conclusions might Nathanael have drawn from the kind of people who seemed to seek out Jesus?

_____

_____

_____

_____

6. What conclusions can you draw about Matthew based on those who were at his house the night Jesus came for dinner?

_____

_____

_____

_____

7. Should we worry about who else they might meet when we consider inviting people into groups where they will also be exposed to the gospel? Why or why not?

_____

_____

_____

_____

⨳ *Imitating the Master* ⨳

Jesus, both Nathanael and Matthew inspire me. I appreciate the way Nathanael owned up to the fact that he was prejudiced. I am moved by Matthew's spontaneous desire to share You with his friends. Thank You that I do not have to reach a certain level of spirituality before I can be an effective witness for You. Thanks, Jesus, for the reminder that You can use me today just as I am. In our Lord Jesus' Name. Amen.

FRIDAY

Read Hebrews 11:33–38.

1. Unlike the early portion of Hebrews 11, no names are given in this section. How does that impact the way you read these verses?

_____

_____

_____

_____

2. What people are you aware of who have suffered in some way for the gospel?

_____

_____

_____

_____

3. What do you admire about them?

_____

_____

4. Does the fact that we know virtually nothing about James the Less, Simon the Zealot, and Judas (not Iscariot) minimize their importance in your mind? Why or why not?

_____

_____

_____

_____

5. What lessons from Judas Iscariot's life stand out in your mind?

_____

_____

_____

_____

6. It appears that Judas Iscariot was motivated by greed and a lust for money. When are you most vulnerable to serving this earthly "god"?

_____

_____

_____

_____

7. Judas threw the money away when he realized that his transaction had been foolish. When have you experienced the emptiness of something you thought you had to have?

_____

_____

_____

_____

❧ *Imitating the Master* ❧

Lord Jesus, it is frightful to think how Judas could have spent so much time with You and witnessed the miracles You did and never come to a place of putting his trust in You. Oh, Lord, don't let me become so familiar with spiritual things that they cease to drive me to my knees in awe and humility.
In our Lord Jesus' Name. Amen.

FOR LEADERS

(Notes and suggested answers for selected questions.)

ANOTHER LOOK

1. Choosing disciples from outside the religious establishment was Jesus' way of judging those who ignored Him and bad-mouthed Him for the first eighteen months of His public ministry.

2. The length of intensive training was not as long as we often think. The reason Jesus opted for a small band of His closest followers was to increase His effectiveness and efficiency in a growing public ministry.

3. The apostles' occupations included, among other things: several fishermen, a political insurrectionist, and a tax collector. All but Judas were from Galilee (the other side of the tracks).

4. Those who were near the top of the list were those who spent the most time with Jesus. The further down in the lists, the less significant those disciples were in terms of influence or leadership.

5. Jesus called James and John "Sons of Thunder" to bring them up short when they were exhibiting wrong behavior. The same is true when He called Peter by the name Simon. But Jesus also called the big fisherman Peter ("Rock") when He was reminding him of his potential.

BIBLICAL CONNECTIONS

6. God chooses the weak things of the world to shame the wise. The reason He uses ordinary, imperfect individuals is so that He receives the glory in all things.

7. Mark's account indicates that Jesus called the disciples to "be with Him" and to send them out. Before they would be in a position to minister to others, it was important that they were ministered to by Jesus. Yes, the order is important and has implications for today's disciples.

8. The Greek seekers represent those we have been called to reach. Philip represents someone with the gift of hospitality. Andrew represents someone with the gift of evangelism (who could introduce the Greeks to Christ). Jesus is the head of the Body as well as the one who individually gifts each person He calls.

9. Paul admits that even though he is a committed follower of Jesus, he is a sinful man capable of doing what he detests. The contradictions in his life cause him to feel like a wretch. His only hope is in Jesus, for whom he is most grateful.

10. This final chapter of John's Gospel is filled with powerful lessons. They include:

    • Jesus' willingness to continue to serve His disciples as a servant, even though they had returned to fishing and had lost sight of their calling to fish for men. He cooked them breakfast on the beach and miraculously caused them to catch a huge number of fish.

    • Jesus expressed love for Peter in spite of the big fisherman's big failure. The Lord allowed Peter to express his loyalty as many times as he had denied Him.

    • Jesus personalized His approach to those who followed Him. He had one plan for Peter's future and another one for John's future. We also see in this chapter the humility of a once arrogant and prideful John who doesn't even mention his own name.

HIGHLIGHTING THE LESSON

11. Since there were twelve tribes of Israel in the Old Testament, this was a symbolic way that Jesus declared that those who followed after Him were to be the new Israel (the true people of God).

12. Simon the Zealot and Matthew the tax collector couldn't have had much in common. One hated the Romans and one had sold out to them. But Jesus was determined to teach them that they were both alike (sinners in need of a Savior) and that they needed each other to fulfill His will for their lives.

13. After being called by Jesus to follow Him, Philip immediately went to his closest friend Nathanael to tell him what had happened and to convince him to join Jesus, too. As soon as Matthew was embraced by Jesus' loving call, he threw a party for his "politically incorrect" friends so that they could meet Him. In addition, Jesus chose two sets of brothers who were friends because of their common fishing enterprise. He knew that their friendship would provide accountability and moral support as they went out with a common cause to reach others.

14. Andrew, Peter, James, and John were quite familiar with the writings of the prophets that spoke of a coming Messiah. That is why they left Galilee to follow John the Baptist. They were grounded in Scripture and were motivated in their search for truth. Philip and Nathanael apparently were also in Judah tracking John the Baptist because of what they had been studying in

the Law of Moses and the Prophets. Because of what they had studied, their decision to leave all to follow Jesus was easier. They were convinced that they had found the One of whom the Scriptures spoke. Matthew (although excluded from the synagogue because of his occupation) had an obvious knowledge of the Old Testament which he incorporated into his Gospel in a big way.

15. Jesus transformed uneducated, fickle commoners into extraordinary examples of commitment and courage. It was obviously the presence of Jesus in their lives that accounted for the change.

Endnotes

Other than noted below, all sidebar quotes are taken from the companion book by John MacArthur, *Twelve Ordinary Men* (Nashville: W Publishing Group, 2002).

LESSON 1

1 John MacArthur, *The MacArthur Study Bible* (Nashville: Word Publishing, 1997), 1579.

LESSON 12

2 MacArthur, *The MacArthur Study Bible* (Nashville: Word Publishing, 1997), 1409.
3 MacArthur, *MacArthur's Quick Reference Guide to the Bible* (Nashville: W Publishing Group, 2001), 185.